SOLITUDE

Aloneness is neutral.

To be alone is simply to be at a distance—

in bathroom or crowded café.

Loneliness is negative.

To be lonely is to dislike being alone,

even to be cramped and embittered by it.

But to be alone or to live alone

is not necessarily something to dread.

For solitude is positive.

To be solitary is not to exclude or be excluded.

It is to be in touch with the springs of your own creativity;

it is to be aware

that we can never be separate from anyone;

it is to know at the deepest level

what it is to love and be loved.

JIM COTTER

ONE LIKE JESUS

Conversations on the Single Life

DEBRA K. FARRINGTON

Loyola Press

Chicago

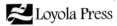
Loyola Press

3441 North Ashland Avenue
Chicago, Illinois 60657

Interior design by Jeanne Calabrese Design

Library of Congress Cataloging-in-Publication Data
Farrington, Debra K.
    One like Jesus : conversations on the single life / Debra K.
  Farrington.
       p.   cm.
    ISBN 0-8294-1267-0 (pbk.)
    1.Single people—Prayer-books and devotions—English. I. Title.
BV4596.S5F37   1999
248.8'4—dc21   98-36978
                                                  CIP

Printed in the United States of America

99 00 01 02 03 / 10 9 8 7 6 5 4 3 2 1

For my dad,
who never asked me when I was going to settle down,
get married, and give him grandchildren.

CONTENTS

FOREWORD BY ALAN JONES   XI

ACKNOWLEDGMENTS   XV

INTRODUCTION   XVII

CHAPTER ONE
JESUS AS ROLE MODEL   1

Jesus, the Ultimate Role Model / Available to All / Being Alone / Jesus and His Friends / Thirteen at the Table / Walking on Water / Jesus' Surrender / Jesus' Anger

CHAPTER TWO

OTHER ROLE MODELS IN SCRIPTURE 19

*Single Role Models from the Bible / Hagar and New Life /
Miriam's Celebration / Elijah and Loving God / Ruth
Chooses Singleness / Rahab's Courage / Jeremiah's Call
to Be Single / Mary's Faithfulness / The Friendship
of Mary and Elizabeth / Anna Prophesies / Jesus Chooses
Mary Magdalene*

CHAPTER THREE

**JOURNEYING FROM EGYPT TO THE
PROMISED LAND** 43

*Cloudy Days / Learning to Be Single / Seeing Jesus /
Gathering Today's Treasures / Becoming All We Are Meant
to Be / Getting Along Together / A Purpose in the Fog /
Journey toward Love / Listening to the Call / Each One
Matters / No Instant Solutions / Planted Where We Belong*

CHAPTER FOUR

MANNA IN THE WILDERNESS 69

*Accepting and Being Manna / Role Models in Our Midst /
Touch / Support Groups / Asking for Help / Nurturing
Communities / Church and Family / Getting Support /
Friends / E-mail / Pets / Life-Saving Medicine / God
Provides / No Clones / God as Manna*

CHAPTER FIVE

BY THE WATERS OF BABYLON   101

*Living in Babylon / God in the Dark / Spouse Stealing /
Anger as a Building Block / Pairs and Spares / Two by Two in
the Ark / Separate at Church / Sharing the Chores / Prince
Charming / Job's Unhelpful Friends*

CHAPTER SIX

SEEING A NEW WAY   123

*Viewed from a Different Angle / A Solitary Christmas /
Eat Dessert First / God Hears / Working / Victimhood vs.
Taking Control / Throw a Party / Burnout / Dating / Sex /
Vacations / Good Soil*

CHAPTER SEVEN

THE NEW JERUSALEM   149

*Enjoyment / Living Alone / Housekeeping, or Not / Children/
Male and Female / Freedom / Travel / Saturday Morning /
Flirtation / Be Here Now*

CHAPTER EIGHT

GOD'S UNCONDITIONAL LOVE   171

*God's Love / God Calls Us by Name / A Stronghold in Times
of Trouble / The Body Holy / Worm Theology / Light of the
World / God's Love Empowers / Claiming God's Love /
God, Not the Knight on a White Horse / Opportunities /
Singleness in Scripture / Knowing Fully / God Loves You*

FOREWORD

A friend of mine translates the opening of the Fourth Gospel in this way: "In the beginning was the conversation." The fullness of truth comes to us only when we are in conversation with each other, with the world, and with the stories and texts that inform our lives. Conversation is a godly activity because when we are open to, and respectful of, one another, when we listen and pay attention to each other, God is glorified. Debra Farrington has not only identified a powerful issue in modern life—the state of being, and (sometimes) the call to be, single—but has also used the perfect form to express her concerns and give encouragement to those who sometimes feel trapped in their single state, trapped by their own inner voices or trapped by the community in which they find themselves. She shows that what some people see as a trap God has sometimes sent as a gift. Conversation is the preferred way to move forward when it comes to matters of the heart, and these meditations help move the reader into a gentle yet challenging place of discernment. God is always trying to reach us.

I am convinced that we are in a time when basic definitions of what it means to be human are being renegotiated —including definitions of our faith-journey. Human history can be interpreted as one story after another of exclusion. It is full of tales about people trying to get into the human conversation. Some do it angrily and noisily. Others actually take over the conversation and make sure those who formerly dominated it are pushed to the edges. Youth is silenced by age, and then youth takes its revenge. One race or tribe dominates another, and then the roles are reversed. Men lord it over women, and women seek to turn the tables. The married have often looked upon the unmarried as second-class, wounded, and incomplete. The silent reproach is "Why can't you be like us? Why can't you be 'normal'?" Or worse, the religious community, by invoking in a twisted way the biblical witness, has sometimes made the single state into something of a curse. Debra Farrington gently and persuasively speaks from her own experience and helps us (whether we are single or not) see the key texts of Scripture in a new light.

In any explanation of human society we should always ask who is excluded from the conversation, who is likely to be rendered invisible. My own experience of God was shaped by a society ruled by class. Yet I was able to move through that to hear a gospel that proclaimed an aristocracy of being. It was romantic and inclusive. I was taught that I am what my brothers and sisters are. If they are lost, then so am I. If they are found, I am found too. I had to ask myself, What is the method by which the excluded can enter a group, change its structure, and give themselves a place at the table? How do we cross the threshold into a previously excluding community? The point is not to terrify us into change but to open us up to who we really are as children of God and, therefore, sisters and brothers to each other. None of us is dispensable—able to be dispensed with—or "good for nothing."

When one thinks of the world community with millions on the move, millions displaced, there's a sense that there is an immigrant child in all of us. This is not to trivialize the agonies and trials of actual immigrants in hostile cultures but to acknowledge that *somos todos mestizos*—we are all of mixed origin. This is as true on the spiritual and psychological levels as on the level of tribe. The old categories don't quite fit anymore. For example, we are beginning to realize that marriage is an institution with a long history that reveals marriage was used for a multitude of purposes, many of them economic and social. When economic and social structures change, the institution of marriage is reordered.

We are made after the image of God, which means that there is a radical and refreshing openness about being human, since God is both inexhaustible and, in one sense, unknowable. So are we! Debra Farrington speaks about the single life in this generous context. It is an awesome and godly thing to be alive, to be human. We are deeper and lovelier than we know. One of the deepest but hardest lessons we have to learn in this, the School of Love, is that intimacy requires solitude. Solidarity requires a true sense of self. If we cannot be alone and at peace with ourselves we can never be truly present to one another. The poet Marianne Moore wrote, "The only cure for loneliness is solitude." It is as if we are playing a never-ending game of hide-and-seek with each other. We need to respect each other with regard to our need to remain hidden, but what a joy it is to be found, even *found out,* and not condemned! This is the gift of the gospel. We learn that being is communion and that "in the beginning was the conversation."

ALAN JONES
DEAN OF GRACE CATHEDRAL
SAN FRANCISCO

ACKNOWLEDGMENTS

Although an author must spend many hours by herself staring at pen and paper and the computer screen in order to bring a book to life, there would be no book without the advice, help, and support of a wide variety of people. *One Like Jesus* is the product not only of my own life experiences, but of the midwifery of some special friends and colleagues.

My thanks to Phyllis Tickle, who, from the very start, nurtured this project. As a friend and fellow author, she has patiently listened to endless and often boring tales of the birth process. Linda Roghaar, my agent, also deserves appreciation for her belief in this project. She says an agent is as much a therapist as a business associate, and I can attest that she has been helpful in both roles. Val Gittings, my colleague and friend, read the manuscript several times and provided helpful suggestions when I got stuck. Her editorial eye, her knowledge of the Bible, and her unflagging support of my writing are deeply appreciated. And finally, thanks to my editor, LaVonne Neff, who saw a raw product with potential. She improved this manuscript immeasurably with her editorial eye, and she knew what I was trying to accomplish with this book even when I did not.

INTRODUCTION

In my mid-twenties I attended a party where a palm-reader was circulating in the crowd. She came up to me at one point, read my palm, and probably told me many things, but I remember hearing only one: that I would marry at age thirty-two. Furthermore, I would marry someone who had been a friend for a long time.

I wouldn't normally visit a palm-reader or put much stock in such predictions, but all of us like hearing of a future that suits us. So I tucked this information about my future marriage away in my head and, without being completely conscious of it, put many parts of my life on hold. I knew they would come to life, magically, when I turned thirty-two.

When I was thirty-one, I began to wonder which of my good friends I was slated to marry. By age thirty-three, still single, I woke up and wondered if it might not be time to get on with my life. I began to buy the household items one would otherwise receive at a wedding shower: blenders, good dishes, living-room and bedroom furniture that I really enjoyed. I also began to look around for resources and support for the single life and found fewer than I would have liked.

Like many others in the baby boomer generation, I left the church as a teenager and didn't come back until I was in my late twenties. When, in my early thirties, I began to look for support for singles, I started with my church. I got very mixed signals. Certainly singles were welcome, at least in some places, but my overriding sense in that community—and in other church communities I have known since—was that singles are a problem for the church.

I am not the first person to notice this phenomenon. In *Singles at the Crossroads,* Albert Hsu quotes one of the most noted of church observers, Lyle Schaller, on the issue of singles in the church: "Schaller ... describes local churches as having many 'doors' which newcomers can walk through to become involved with the church. The door for couples and families may be wide open, but the door for singles may seem shut tight, with a 'hand-lettered sign tacked to the door which declares Temporarily Closed: Come Back When You're Married and Have Two Children.' "[1]

The church has a problem with singles, and it needs to face up to it — quickly. The reality today is this: Most of us will be single at some point in our adult lives, whether for a period of time before we first marry, or because of divorce or the death of a spouse, or because we never married. And more of us are single now than at any previous time in American history. In 1970, according to the Census Bureau, 28 percent of the adult population was single, compared to 4 percent during the Colonial period. By 1988 the percentage had grown to 37. Today, almost half of adult Americans are single. The average age for first marriage has increased and is now in the late twenties. High divorce rates continue to swell the single population. If for no other reason, the numbers alone suggest that it is important for the church to begin to formulate a theology around being single, one that affirms and celebrates single people, one that welcomes them into the Christian life and the life of the church.

The meditations on the following pages, written primarily to support and encourage singles, are also an effort to begin to sketch that theology. This is by no means an exhaustive attempt, and I make no claims of being a theologian. Nonetheless, certain elements of an emerging picture of Christian singleness can be seen in the pieces that follow. These elements include the following affirmations:

1. *The Bible sanctions singleness as a fulfilling and important way of living.*

Both the Hebrew Scriptures and the New Testament contain examples of single people with important ministries. We can find models for elements of the single life in Jeremiah, Elijah, Jesus, Paul, Mary Magdalene, Mary, Martha, Lazarus, and others.

2. *God loves each of us just as we are.*
   The Bible is full of God's love for humanity, stressing it over and over again. Nowhere in the Bible does it say that God loves us better when we are married. We are not incomplete halves that God will love better when made whole. God loves us deeply and unconditionally right this moment.

3. *God created a world full of wonderful things and opportunities, and we are meant to enjoy them.*
   Many of us believe we must postpone living life to the fullest until we are married. Repeatedly, however, Scripture tells of the rich rewards, both material and spiritual, of this life. God intends for all of us to avail ourselves of the riches provided. This does not mean that we selfishly exploit people and things for our own purposes. But neither should we turn away from the great gifts that God gives us.

4. *God is present with us in our suffering and anger.*
   We may feel deeply wounded by our experiences as single people. God does not will these hurts upon us, but is with us in our pain and suffering. God's will is for a righteous world where everyone is valued equally.

5. *God may have ministries for some of us that are more effectively accomplished by single people.*

   Though not all single people are necessarily called to be single, some of us may indeed be called to a ministry that would be much more difficult with a spouse or family.

One difficulty for singles and for the church today is a lack of understanding about the life passages experienced by singles. Since almost every adult development model created by psychologists assumes that adults are married, these models are difficult to apply to single adults. Today's high percentage of singles is a relatively new phenomenon, and so singles are currently forging their own paths and redefining what it means to be single within the culture and within the church. As one of those singles, I have identified some broad stages in the single experience and have arranged these meditations accordingly.

The first thing many of us need is a role model, and the first two chapters—"Jesus as Role Model" and "Other Role Models in Scripture"—look at Jesus and other biblical figures who can show us how we might live.

Chapter 3, "Journeying from Egypt to the Promised Land," looks at the journey from wherever we are today to a life that is more fulfilling. It deals with the joys and dangers of wandering in the desert for a while as we begin to learn who we are and what we are meant to be.

While we wander, God provides manna and water to sustain us. Those things that feed and support us are the subject of chapter 4, "Manna in the Wilderness."

No journey comes without elements of darkness and difficulty. We have periods of discouragement and despair when we wonder if we will ever be happy again. In chapter 5, "By the Waters of Babylon," we explore the dark times of exile and loss.

Light often dawns when we start seeing a new way, when we re-vision our circumstances and our problems. Chapter 6, "Seeing a New Way," explores ways in which we might do that.

Finally we come to see our life differently. We begin to live fully at this very moment, and we no longer need to wait for anything else to complete us. The joys of new life are celebrated in chapter 7, "The New Jerusalem."

Chapter 8, "God's Unconditional Love," is the final chapter in placement, but it is the building block of the entire book. God loves us as we are, right this moment, with no ifs, ands, or buts. Many of us have a hard time actually believing that message, but coming to know deep in our souls that God really does love us, unconditionally and with no reservations, is the true and final end of our journey.

It is of course impossible to cover every circumstance of being single. I have tried to be as inclusive as possible, to look at the particular problems of the always-single and the previously married. But because of the unique circumstances that accompany single parenting, I have not tried to deal with issues specifically related to that topic. Single parents will find within these pages meditations that address their feelings about being single, but not about parenting. Parenting is a large and important topic that deserves its own treatment.

I hope that the meditations in this book can be read and used by singles who are ready to hear their own story in the biblical texts, and by those who know them, love them, minister to them, and wish to be supportive. We each bring a different set of expectations, anxieties, and hopes to the single life, informed by the culture, by the church, and by our own histories. These meditations address a wide variety of circumstances and make lots of different suggestions and recommendations for re-visioning the single life. Certainly not all of them will suit each individual reader, and readers should feel free to take what is useful and discard the rest.

If you are single, I hope you will find here some of your own feelings and experiences affirmed, your anger and frustrations expressed, your joys proclaimed. Most of all, I hope you will walk away from reading this knowing more fully how much God loves you just as you are.

---

[1] Lyle Schaller, *Assimilating New Members* (Nashville: Abingdon, 1978), p. 82, quoted in Albert Y. Hsu, *Singles at the Crossroads: A Fresh Perspective on Christian Singleness* (Downers Grove, Ill.: InterVarsity, 1997), p. 126.

CHAPTER ONE
JESUS AS ROLE MODEL

JESUS, THE ULTIMATE ROLE MODEL

And the Word became flesh and lived among us, and
we have seen his glory, the glory as of a father's only
son, full of grace and truth. . . . From his fullness we
have all received, grace upon grace. The law indeed
was given through Moses; grace and truth came
through Jesus Christ.

JOHN 1:14, 16–17

As Christians we look upon Jesus as the ultimate
role model. As single Christians, perhaps we do this with even
more interest. Jesus is, after all, the most notable single person
in the New Testament. More than any other biblical role
model, he brings together all our concerns into one life.

Jesus models God's love for all people by eating with the
"best" and "worst" that society has to offer. Everyone has
access to Jesus: he is equally comfortable with men and
women, rich and poor. Operating largely outside of religious
institutions, Jesus gathers around him the ordinary people,
teaching them, feeding them, and praying with and for them.
Jesus also models courage in the face of death and the hardships of life. Like us, he faces many of these trials on his own,
as do we all ultimately: no one can resist temptation for us;
no one else can die our death. But Jesus is also an example of

the connection we all share, the community that is available to all of us. Jesus must die his own death on the cross, but some of his friends are there to witness this; and though Jesus questions God from the cross, he also knows that God is with him in the end.

We may be single, and we may need to do many things for ourselves, but none of us is ever alone.

How can you be one like Jesus?

Now there was a woman who had been suffering
from hemorrhages for twelve years; and though she
had spent all she had on physicians, no one could
cure her. She came up behind him and touched the
fringe of his clothes, and immediately her hem-
orrhage stopped. Then Jesus asked, "Who touched
me?" When all denied it, Peter said, "Master, the
crowds surround you and press in on you." But
Jesus said, "Someone touched me; for I noticed that
power had gone out from me." When the woman
saw that she could not remain hidden, she came
trembling; and falling down before him, she declared
in the presence of all the people why she had touched
him, and how she had been immediately healed. He
said to her, "Daughter, your faith has made you well;
go in peace."

LUKE 8:43–48

One of the most amazing things about Jesus was
that everyone had access to him. He seemed to have enough
love and enough healing to go around to everyone in need.
Even this woman, considered unclean—religiously taboo—
since she had been hemorrhaging for twelve years, was welcome. She came forth very fearfully when she could hide no

longer, but Jesus, on hearing her story, commended her and bade her go in peace.

I have a long way to go before I am like Jesus in this way. When I find myself in the middle of a very busy day at work and someone who just wants to talk calls me, it can take all my willpower to stop for a few moments and listen to the need behind the call. Like Jesus, I know I have been stopped in my tracks, and it takes a few moments to find out who touched me and why. I have to take a deep breath, put aside my work, and really listen to the caller.

When I am able to do that, the reward is great. Sometimes people just want to share a wonderful moment in their life, while other times they need to tell of something painful. Whatever the situation, being able to listen, to share that experience with someone, is a great privilege.

"Your faith has made you well," Jesus said to this woman whose name we never learn. I hope that, as the years go on, I can be more like Jesus in being available to those who need me—that those who call me in moments of need find that they are healed and restored in some way. I hope that I too, like Jesus, can bid them to go in peacefulness as a result of our time together.

How can you be Jesus to someone today?

BEING ALONE

> Immediately he made the disciples get into the boat
> and go on ahead to the other side, while he dismissed
> the crowds. And after he had dismissed the crowds,
> he went up the mountain by himself to pray. When
> evening came, he was there alone.
>
> MATTHEW 14:22–23

For me, one of the great joys in living alone is the peace and quiet I can experience in the morning when I rise, at the end of the workday when I come home, or on weekends. I don't need the house to be quiet all the time, but I treasure its peacefulness. It feels like a place of retreat.

My work life is so busy. I am with people all day long, talking in person or on the phone. I travel a lot and am surrounded by crowds and by people who need my attention or services. Like Jesus, I need a break from all the activity, from all the demands of those around me. I love coming home to peace and quiet, to an environment in which the noise I hear is within my own control. I can make phone calls if I want, or I can turn on the answering machine and ignore the phone. The stereo plays whatever I wish at my command. The television is on if I want it to be, and otherwise it is silent. And I can go to my prayer corner and sit quietly with God when it suits me.

I struggle hard to follow Jesus in so many ways, but this is not one of them. Like Jesus, I enjoy going off to be alone— for prayer or just refreshment of my body and soul. It is only by being alone some of the time that I am happy being with others the rest of the time.

How does the time you spend alone nourish you?

When Mary came where Jesus was and saw him, she knelt at his feet and said to him, "Lord, if you had been here, my brother would not have died." When Jesus saw her weeping, and the Jews who came with her also weeping, he was greatly disturbed in spirit and deeply moved. He said, "Where have you laid him?" They said to him, "Lord, come and see." Jesus began to weep.

JOHN 11:32-35

This is one of two New Testament stories of the friendship between Mary, Martha, Lazarus, and Jesus. In the first, in Luke 10, Jesus is staying at the home of these three siblings. In this scene, they have sent for Jesus because Lazarus is dying. By the time Jesus arrives, Lazarus is dead. Martha goes out to meet Jesus first, and now Mary goes to him, heartbroken at the death of her brother. Jesus responds to their grief with his own tears. He is a friend to Mary and Martha, and he feels their sorrow.

The friendship of Jesus, Mary, Martha, and Lazarus is a wonderful model for me. We don't know much about the friendship between Jesus and Lazarus, but we can tell that it is deep enough for Jesus to come (even belatedly) when he hears that Lazarus is dying. We get a better sense of the friendship between Mary and Martha and Jesus, a friendship that crosses the gender line. Their friendship is tight and binding, and they can call on one another in their need. The sorrow of Mary and Martha is Jesus' sorrow as well, and I suspect that their joy is his joy too.

These are the sorts of friendships I value in my own life. Friends of the same and opposite sex bring important perspectives into my life. Their presence in moments of great joy and of great sorrow has been a continual blessing to me, and I hope I have been a blessing to them too. Mary, Martha, and Lazarus surely learned about the love of God through their friendship with Jesus. May we all be so lucky as to have friends who, like Jesus, can help us see the unconditional love of God ever more clearly.

What blessings do friends bring to your life?

> So they went and found everything as he had told
> them; and they prepared the Passover meal. When
> the hour came, he took his place at the table, and the
> apostles with him.
>
> LUKE 22:13–14

Have you ever counted the number of people pictured in famous paintings of the Last Supper? Twelve apostles and Jesus, which equals thirteen. Any host in his or her right mind would instantly recognize that we have a serious social faux pas here: an uneven number of guests at the table. Now perhaps this can be pardoned since we have only men in the painting (though I wonder if that was the case in real life) and not a table of even numbers of men and women, carefully seated in alternating order. But in all the Gospel stories of feasts and meals that Jesus attends, he never once worries about whether the numbers of men and women are even.

So many singles experience the tyranny of this even-number social rule. It is particularly difficult for those who are divorced or who have lost a spouse to death. Suddenly they are no longer welcome at dinner parties, or they are invited along with an appropriately single man or woman in order to make the arrangements correct. Invitations come in the mail for so-and-so and a date, not just for the single person alone. While I think the intention is to make us comfortable in a couples' world—by inviting a date, making us a couple—the unwritten assumption is that we are uncomfortable alone. But perhaps the reality is that others are uncomfortable if we are alone.

Jesus never worried about bringing a date, or about the number of people invited to the table, so why should we?

How do you feel about going out alone?

Peter answered him, "Lord, if it is you, command me to come to you on the water." He said, "Come." So Peter got out of the boat, started walking on the water, and came toward Jesus. But when he noticed the strong wind, he became frightened, and beginning to sink, he cried out, "Lord, save me!" Jesus immediately reached out his hand and caught him, saying to him, "You of little faith, why did you doubt?"

MATTHEW 14:28–31

Peter's experience is very much like that of the newly single, or single again. Whether we have been divorced or a spouse has died, we find ourselves walking in unfamiliar places, asked to do things that seem impossible. Navigating the single life again, something we thought we would never have to do, is like being asked to walk across the water.

But this story from Matthew offers some comfort in the journey, for it is Jesus who watches us and waits for us as we explore something completely new. Peter, initially with a great deal of faith, trusts that Jesus will keep him safe as he crosses the water, and he does well at the start. So do some of us who are newly single. We begin to discover some of the joys of our new life, even amidst the sorrows that brought us to this place. But inevitably, the winds begin to blow, and doubt sets in. We wish to be doing something else. Then, just as we begin to sink, Jesus reaches out a hand to us, catches us, and brings us to safety.

Jesus must have known Peter's walk across the water would be difficult in places, just as I think Jesus knows our walk will be hard some days. It is difficult adjusting to being single when all of our life's plans have focused on being part of a couple. Nonetheless, Jesus watches us carefully and is there when we really need a hand to guide us. We have no choice but to follow the path ahead of us, at least for now. But perhaps we can walk with our hand outstretched, knowing that we will be guided when the way gets particularly rough.

What makes you doubt that you can be fulfilled as a single person?

JESUS' SURRENDER

They went to a place called Gethsemane; and he said
to his disciples, "Sit here while I pray." He took with
him Peter and James and John, and began to be
distressed and agitated. And he said to them, "I am
deeply grieved, even to death; remain here, and
keep awake." And going a little farther, he threw
himself on the ground and prayed that, if it were
possible, the hour might pass from him. He said,
"Abba, Father, for you all things are possible; remove
this cup from me; yet, not what I want, but what
you want."

MARK 14:32–36

It is hard for me to imagine the courage of Jesus in
uttering the line, "Remove this cup from me; yet, not what I
want, but what you want." Jesus knows what is ahead, and he
struggles with that. He becomes agitated and distressed,
deeply grieved. The solution for him, as for us, is prayer. Jesus
throws himself on the ground and prays hard. That does not
change what is to come, but it makes the journey bearable for
Jesus. His prayers, his surrender to what God calls him to do,
make it possible to move ahead.

I make no claims to having anything approaching the faith
of Jesus, but I once caught a glimpse of the power of this kind

of prayer. I received a call from my doctor with news about a condition that was potentially life-threatening. Three weeks later, I learned that there was nothing to worry about, but the time between the first phone call and the final test was very difficult for me. Friends and medical teams were incredibly supportive and helpful during that time, but prayer was also essential. Through sustained prayer during those days, I began to understand that God was with me no matter what. God was making all things manageable, even death.

In his prayer at Gethsemane, Jesus models for us a powerful surrender. All things are possible, he reminds God, but do what you believe is best. It takes a lot of strength to pray that prayer of Jesus, even if we pray it in response to fatigue or simple despair. Whenever and however this prayer comes to us during hard days, it is a gift. It is the beginning of a powerful new relationship with God.

Can you really imagine praying, "Not my will, Lord, but yours"?

JESUS' ANGER

In the temple he found people selling cattle, sheep, and doves, and the money changers seated at their tables. Making a whip of cords, he drove all of them out of the temple, both the sheep and the cattle. He also poured out the coins of the money changers and overturned their tables. He told those who were selling the doves, "Take these things out of here! Stop making my Father's house a marketplace!"

JOHN 2:14-16

I'm so glad that Jesus was able to be angry when he needed to be. Some writers have rewritten the Gospels and removed all the passages such as these, which they consider "unworthy" of the real Jesus. They have made Jesus all sweet and cheerful, never angry or frustrated. For me, that takes away some of the richness of Jesus. It erases the prophet who angrily struck out against those who oppressed others or used God's name for evil or financial purposes.

We need the angry Jesus as much as we need the healing Jesus—the Jesus who ate with anyone, an act that appalled those of his day; the healer who broke the rules and healed the sick in the temple on the Sabbath; the fearless man who strode into the temple and overturned the tables of the money changers, who were profaning the holy building. We need this angry Jesus because life is not so different now. We still have the homeless and the downtrodden, and someone must eat with them. People are still suffering everywhere, and we must find ways to heal their pain. And there are still those who would choose profit over the care of souls and bodies. Like Jesus, we must find the courage to overturn their tables.

We need the Jesus who was not afraid to fight for what is right and just. If we erase him from our Gospels, we lose one of the most important aspects of his ministry. We may then lose the courage to fight for the freedom of all. We may forget how to yell, "Stop!"

Sometimes anger is a bridge to compassion.

How do you feel about the angry Jesus?

CHAPTER TWO
OTHER ROLE MODELS IN SCRIPTURE

SINGLE ROLE MODELS FROM THE BIBLE

Let us now sing the praises of famous men,
   our ancestors in their generations.
The Lord apportioned to them great glory,
   his majesty from the beginning.

SIRACH 44:1-2

When we think of our ancestors in the Bible, we often think in pairs. Famous couples leap to mind: Adam and Eve, Abraham and Sarah, Mary and Joseph. But there are single people in the Bible as well. The one who comes most easily to mind is, of course, Jesus. But many of Jesus' friends and disciples were also single: Mary Magdalene, Mary and Martha, and Lazarus. The apostle Paul was very vocal about the advantages of being single. There are also single people in the Hebrew Scriptures. Miriam, Moses' sister, was single, and so were some of the prophets, such as Jeremiah and Elijah.

I see the Bible as the book where most of the wisdom to lead our lives can be found. And so it is possible to find in Scripture clues and suggestions for the single life. Look at the virtues modeled by singles: the initiative of Paul as he traveled through the Roman Empire. Or the wonderful courage of Miriam, who, as a young girl, found a nurse for Moses, and then helped Moses lead the people from Egypt. The generosity of the poor widow who gave most of what she had. The leadership of Lydia, who began the church at Philippi. From Jesus, perhaps the most famous single person in the Bible, we can learn about a life of love, healing, and sacrifice that we, too, can imitate. All these and more model for us the productive, meaningful lives and ministries we can have as single people.

Do any of these biblical role models speak to you? Why?

HAGAR AND NEW LIFE

So she said to Abraham, "Cast out this slave woman with her son. . . ." The matter was very distressing to Abraham on account of his son. But God said to Abraham, "Do not be distressed . . . ; whatever Sarah says to you, do as she tells you, for it is through Isaac that offspring shall be named for you. As for the son of the slave woman, I will make a nation of him also, because he is your offspring." So Abraham rose early in the morning, and took bread and a skin of water, and gave it to Hagar, putting it on her shoulder, along with the child, and sent her away.

GENESIS 21:10–14

Hagar's story is one of the more difficult ones in the Bible. Sarah, unable to have a child, sends Abraham to Hagar, Sarah's slave, who conceives a child by him. Tensions then run so high between Hagar and Sarah that Hagar runs away, coming back only when God instructs her to do so. Later, when Sarah has given birth to Isaac, she demands that Abraham send Hagar away entirely. Hagar must wander the desert with little food and water, fearing for her own life and for the life of her child, Ishmael. God, however, has other plans for Ishmael. A well full of water appears to Hagar, and they survive their ordeal.

There are many interpretations of Hagar's story. Theologian Phyllis Trible labels it one of the "texts of terror" in the Bible.[1] Miriam Therese Winter, on the other hand, suggests that perhaps Sarah did Hagar a favor by sending her out into the desert, since the journey began a new life for Hagar.[2] For singles, perhaps there is an element of truth in both of these interpretations.

Hagar, like many singles, lives in difficult circumstances, and her exile to the desert simply seems like a continuation of that. Still, leaving Abraham and Sarah means leaving slavery. It is an opportunity to escape miserable living conditions and begin again. And so, Hagar offers us great hope. She felt as if she was being sent into the desert to die, but she found that God had other plans for her. Perhaps some of us who feel exiled in our singleness will find, like Hagar, that God has better plans for us. Difficult circumstances can be invitations to new life.

What have been the times in your life when difficulties turned into invitations?

---

[1] *Texts of Terror* (Minneapolis: Fortress, 1984).
[2] *Womanwisdom* (New York: Crossroad, 1991), p. 38.

MIRIAM'S CELEBRATION

When the horses of Pharaoh with his chariots and his chariot drivers went into the sea, the LORD brought back the waters of the sea upon them; but the Israelites walked through the sea on dry ground. Then the prophet Miriam, Aaron's sister, took a tambourine in her hand; and all the women went out after her with tambourines and with dancing. And Miriam sang to them: "Sing to the LORD, for he has triumphed gloriously; horse and rider he has thrown into the sea."

EXODUS 15:19–21

Miriam is the first female prophet of the Hebrew Scriptures. Sister to Moses and Aaron, she helps them lead the people out of Egypt and through the desert. Her life is not an easy one. She wanders in the desert for years with Moses. When she and Aaron criticize Moses, God inflicts Miriam with leprosy. Still, the people love her and pay her great respect.

Miriam loves God, even in the difficult times. And this moment of wild celebration is one of her most exhilarating moments in the Bible. It may seem a little bloodthirsty to us today to celebrate the death of the Egyptians, but you have to admire Miriam's utter abandon in praising God. She picks up her tambourine and begins to dance, and all the women join in. She doesn't utter a quiet little prayer of thanks to God under her breath. She dances and sings for everyone to hear, and she invites everyone around her to do likewise.

I admire Miriam. I am not nearly so brave about praising God. Praying quietly (perhaps even under my breath) a brief prayer of thanks is often more my speed. But Miriam gives me courage to just belt out a prayer of thanks occasionally, to sing loudly, to dance, to shout. If Miriam can praise God with abandon, so can I.

What might cause you to belt out a prayer of thanks to God?

ELIJAH AND LOVING GOD

After this the son of the woman, the mistress of the
house, became ill; his illness was so severe that there
was no breath left in him. She then said to Elijah,
"What have you against me, O man of God? You have
come to me to bring my sin to remembrance, and
to cause the death of my son!" But he said to her,
"Give me your son." He took him from her bosom,
carried him up into the upper chamber where he
was lodging, and laid him on his own bed. He cried
out to the LORD, "O LORD my God, have you brought
calamity even upon the widow with whom I am
staying, by killing her son?". . . The LORD listened to
the voice of Elijah; the life of the child came into him
again, and he revived.

1 KINGS 17:17–20, 22

Elijah, one of the better-known prophets of the
Hebrew Scriptures, was a single man. As with many prophets,
he was known primarily for his angry prophesying against
his own people who worshiped false gods. He wasn't necessarily the kind of person we might enjoy having as a next-
door neighbor. On the other hand, he was a man of extraor-
dinary compassion, as we read in this story.

During a time of drought and famine, God sends Elijah to stay in a widow's house. God gives the widow food enough for Elijah, herself, and her son. When the son becomes ill and dies, Elijah intercedes and passionately begs God to reward the widow's faithfulness by bringing her son back to life. God does so.

We do not often think of Elijah's compassionate side. We focus more on his anger and his courage in dangerous circumstances. But Elijah, like us, is a complex person, filled with both anger and love. All the feelings he experiences, however, seem to come from the same place: from his love of God and his confidence in the path God has set for him.

May we be like Elijah in that way, with our anger and love rising from our love of God, from God's love for us, and from walking on the pathway we have been given. Compassion and anger are both ways of loving God.

How does your own love of God fuel both your compassion and your anger?

RUTH CHOOSES SINGLENESS

But Naomi said to her two daughters-in-law, "Go back each of you to your mother's house. May the LORD deal kindly with you, as you have dealt with the dead and with me. The LORD grant that you may find security, each of you in the house of your husband." . . . Then they wept aloud again. Orpah kissed her mother-in-law, but Ruth clung to her.

So she said, "See, your sister-in-law has gone back to her people and to her gods; return after your sister-in-law." But Ruth said, "Do not press me to leave you or to turn back from following you! Where you go, I will go."

RUTH 1:8–9, 14–16

After the deaths of the husbands of Naomi, Ruth, and Orpah, Naomi sends her two daughters-in-law away, encouraging them to find security in the form of new husbands. She can imagine no other possibility for them. The sooner they remarry, the better. But Ruth refuses to leave, rejecting the most obvious and accepted path. Though she eventually remarries, she has no way of knowing that this will happen when she chooses to remain with Naomi.

It must be very tempting to jump back into marriage after losing a partner, particularly one that was much loved, to death or divorce. It isn't my purpose to criticize those decisions, for some are very happy with their new marriages. But I applaud the courage of Ruth as well, as she made a decision to live a life unfamiliar to her. She deliberately chose to live as a stranger among those who were not her people, to travel with another single woman into unknown territory, with no husband in sight. And in the process, she discovered that she could care for herself and for her mother-in-law. She became a richer and fuller person. Perhaps, when she did remarry, she brought greater gifts to her second husband as the result of her growth as a single person.

In what ways are you becoming a richer or fuller person?

RAHAB'S COURAGE

Then Joshua son of Nun sent two men secretly from
Shittim as spies, saying, "Go, view the land, especially
Jericho." So they went, and entered the house of
a prostitute whose name was Rahab, and spent the
night there. The king of Jericho was told, "Some
Israelites have come here tonight to search out the
land." Then the king of Jericho sent orders to Rahab,
"Bring out the men who have come to you, who
entered your house, for they have come only to
search out the whole land." But the woman took the
two men and hid them. Then she said, "True, the
men came to me, but I did not know where they
came from. And when it was time to close the gate
at dark, the men went out. Where the men went
I do not know. Pursue them quickly, for you can
overtake them."

JOSHUA 2:1–5

Does this seem like an odd story to hold up as a
model for singles? Rahab, after all, is a prostitute, and in the
process of saving Joshua's men, she lies. That would seem to
make her an unlikely role model. But then again, there isn't a
role model in the world who is perfect in all ways. Rahab's

other characteristics—her courage, her quick thinking, her deal making—do seem admirable.

Rahab hides Joshua's men because she knows that God has sent them to scout out the new land God intends for the Israelites. She lies and protects them out of faithfulness, much as people once hid runaway slaves in this country, and Jews from the Nazis during World War II. She does this with courage, knowing that if she is caught she can be severely punished. She does this because she knows it is right.

Her courage doesn't stop with hiding the spies. For her bravery she turns around and demands a deal—that when Joshua and his army come back to conquer Jericho, they must spare her and her father, mother, brothers, and other family members. As a friend of mine says, she made a deal that worked for her and for God at the same time.

So I like Rahab. She doesn't need a husband to help her negotiate; she herself is complete and able. She simply does what needs to be done without wavering, and she is not afraid to make a bargain in return for her help. Rahab is a single person worth admiring.

Is there something in your life that would benefit from Rahab's courage?

JEREMIAH'S CALL TO BE SINGLE

The word of the Lord came to me: You shall not
take a wife, nor shall you have sons or daughters
in this place.

JEREMIAH 16:1-2

Jeremiah is one of the few people in the Bible who
seem to have been called to the single life. The life of a
prophet was hard and dangerous, so perhaps God was telling
Jeremiah that he needed to focus all of his energy on the tasks
at hand and avoid distractions. No compromises were possible in Jeremiah's life; his job description was clear.

I wonder what would have happened if Jeremiah had had
a wife. Today it is not unusual for each member of a married
couple to be employed in a job that is fulfilling and financially important to the pair. When one or the other partner
wants to take a new job, many couples find themselves taking turns with career moves, particularly those that entail relocation. Priority will be given first to one person's career, and
then the other's. Can you just see Jeremiah with a hypothetical wife when God calls Jeremiah to go prophesy? Would
Jeremiah have said, "Sorry, God, but it's Lydia's turn for a
career move. Have you got something local for me instead?"

Compromise is often necessary, but one of the great joys of the single life is not having to compromise in this way. We are free, as was Jeremiah, to do what we sense God calls us to do without worrying about how it affects a spouse.

What does God call you to do while you are single?

> Now the birth of Jesus the Messiah took place in this way. When his mother Mary had been engaged to Joseph, but before they lived together, she was found to be with child from the Holy Spirit. Her husband Joseph, being a righteous man and unwilling to expose her to public disgrace, planned to dismiss her quietly.
>
> MATTHEW 1:18–19

Often when we hear Mary's story and her wonderful Magnificat in Luke 1, we focus on her bravery in saying yes to God. Being pregnant, and not by Joseph, opens Mary to tremendous disgrace, and she is indeed very courageous to accept the role asked of her.

But Mary risks even more than the disgrace of an illegitimate pregnancy here. She risks being single. Joseph is well within his rights to send her away, leaving her permanently single and without any place in society. But Mary would rather say yes to God and endure the disdain of those around her than walk away from God's call.

There are many ways in which we may be asked to make a choice for being single. A spouse being abused has to make the hard choice to leave. A single pregnant woman can be faced with deciding to marry versus raising a child alone. Someone with a terminally ill spouse may need to let go emotionally so that the dying loved one can go peacefully. Often we must make those choices without knowing what lies ahead, though we can be sure that it will not be easy at times. Mary did not end up single, though her decision could have easily led to that. She was willing, however, to face disgrace and pain if that was the road God chose for her.

Are you willing to be single if that is God's call to you?

THE FRIENDSHIP OF MARY
AND ELIZABETH

In those days Mary set out and went with haste to a
Judean town in the hill country, where she entered
the house of Zechariah and greeted Elizabeth. When
Elizabeth heard Mary's greeting, the child leaped in
her womb.... And Mary remained with her about
three months and then returned to her home.

LUKE 1:39–41, 56

I love this story of friendship between Mary and
Elizabeth. Both women are experiencing something quite unexpected. Elizabeth is old and barren and hadn't expected to
be pregnant. And Mary is pregnant under unconventional
circumstances. Elizabeth, who has been shamed by her bar-
renness all her life, is about to become acceptable. Mary, who
has lived respectably as a betrothed virgin, is about to
become unacceptable. They share a sense of amazement; their
lives are not going as planned. And so they come together and
spend three months sharing their unusual stories with each
other, finding comfort and delight in each other's presence.

We can learn something from these two women. So many
of us have deep wounds, and we shy away from any conversation that might expose them. We are afraid that if we speak

about our anger or frustration we will be rejected by others. We are afraid to be labeled "bitter" or "pathetic." So we remain quiet, and our wounds fester.

But we need to be more like Mary and Elizabeth if we are to be happy and whole human beings. We need to talk with others about our painful and positive experiences. Each of us longs to know that others share our journey, that our voices are heard, that others feel as we do. Perhaps we need to find the courage of Mary and Elizabeth to tell someone our unusual stories. In telling them, we may find they are not as unspeakable as we thought.

With whom can you share your stories?

ANNA PROPHESIES

There was also a prophet, Anna the daughter of
Phanuel, of the tribe of Asher. She was of a great
age, having lived with her husband seven years after
her marriage, then as a widow to the age of eighty-
four. She never left the temple but worshiped
there with fasting and prayer night and day. At that
moment she came, and began to praise God and
to speak about the child to all who were looking for
the redemption of Jerusalem.

LUKE 2:36–38

Many passages in the Bible paint a rather
bleak picture for widows. Often they are equated with
orphans, with those who are helpless and require assistance if
they are to survive at all. No doubt that reflects a social reality in biblical times, but it is a relief to find, in Anna, a different picture of widowhood.

Anna, after being married for a brief time, is widowed,
and she chooses not to remarry. In those days, of course, she
had few choices about where to go and what to do as an unmarried woman, and Anna chooses to remain in the temple
focusing her life on serving God. Perhaps as a result of her
closeness to God, she is given knowledge of the child Jesus,

and she prophesies of him to the people who are gathered in the temple.

Anna reminds me of a friend of mine. She is divorced and is the single parent of one child. Though she did not want the divorce originally, she acknowledges that she likes who she has become in the last few years. She is stronger, more capable, more sure of herself, and she wonders if these changes would have happened had she stayed in an unhappy marriage. Like Anna, my friend has grown in knowing herself and God, and as a result she is more what she feels God calls her to be. She sees and speaks more clearly than she did in the past.

What gifts are you finding in the single life?

JESUS CHOOSES MARY MAGDALENE

But Mary stood weeping outside the tomb. As she
wept, she bent over to look into the tomb; and she
saw two angels in white, sitting where the body of
Jesus had been lying, one at the head and the other
at the feet. They said to her, "Woman, why are you
weeping?" She said to them, "They have taken away
my Lord, and I do not know where they have laid
him." When she had said this, she turned around and
saw Jesus standing there.

JOHN 20:11–14

In all of the Gospels Mary Magdalene is the first, or
among the first, to see the resurrected Christ. A woman, and
a single woman at that—one of the lowest of the low in biblical times—was chosen as the one to see Christ first and to
go tell others. Rather than choose to reveal himself to someone the culture would recognize as important, Jesus reverses
cultural expectations and appears to an unmarried woman.

This passage leads me to believe that God calls all of us to
important ministries, no matter how poor we imagine ourselves to be. I make no claims to understand how God's will
works in this world. But I am convinced that God loves us
and that God calls each one of us to a ministry that only we

can fulfill. Jesus chose to reveal himself to Mary Magdalene rather than to someone others would recognize as more powerful. Jesus often reversed the expectations of those in his society by noticing and choosing to be with those deemed unworthy. But Jesus' attention to the poor and powerless, as well as to the wealthy and powerful, can remind us that those categories are of our own making, and not God's.

In what ways have you put yourself and others in categories not of God's making?

CHAPTER THREE
JOURNEYING FROM EGYPT TO THE PROMISED LAND

CLOUDY DAYS

On the day the tabernacle was set up, the cloud
covered the tabernacle, the tent of the covenant;
and from evening until morning it was over
the tabernacle, having the appearance of fire.
It was always so: the cloud covered it by day and
the appearance of fire by night. Whenever the
cloud lifted from over the tent, then the Israelites
would set out; and in the place where the cloud
settled down, there the Israelites would camp.

NUMBERS 9:15-17

Having left the bondage of Egypt, the Israelites
wandered for years in the desert, living in hopes of finding the
Promised Land. The journey was difficult. Food and water
were scarce, and life without a home was hard. During their
second year in the desert God commanded the Israelites to
celebrate the Passover, and to do this, they set up the tabernacle. A cloud descended over it and governed the Israelites'
movement and rest periods.

I like the symbolism of this story from the Hebrew
Scriptures. When the cloud descends and covers the tent, the
people stay put. The cloud by day and fire by night obscure
their path, their access to the tabernacle, and so they stay

where they are. They do not try to move forward or go on with their journey. When the cloud lifts, when they can see again, they are ready to continue.

Often when my life is clouded, I try to forge ahead anyway, though it rarely works. It is too hard to see my way through thick clouds, and I end up losing ground rather than gaining anything. Or I end up off course entirely and have no idea where I am. It is so hard for me to be patient when the cloud surrounds me. I do not want to wait for a clear day, for clarity—I just want to get on to the next thing. I need to be more like the Israelites and just rest in camp when the cloud is present. I need to learn to enjoy the Sabbath rest that the cloud provides.

What is your response when clouds descend on you?

LEARNING TO BE SINGLE

Let me hear of your steadfast love in the morning,
    for in you I put my trust.
Teach me the way I should go,
    for to you I lift up my soul.

PSALM 143:8

None of us is born knowing how to be single. Most of us are born into families, and as children we live in a group situation of some sort. We rely on others—adults and caretakers—to help us, nurture us, and give us support. Many of us never taste life on our own until we leave high school or college. Those who marry early may not experience anything of singleness even then. But most of us will be single at some point in our life, by choice or circumstance, and few of us are actually prepared for that.

I first faced the single life right out of college. I continued to work in the town where I'd attended college, but most of my friends had graduated and were gone. I felt very much at a loss when I began living on my own. I was faced with being my own caretaker for the first time, with shopping and cooking, setting up housekeeping, making a living and supporting myself, making all of my own decisions. And I discovered what many of us do, that our own resources are not sufficient to the task. We try to be superhuman, to manage our home and work lives seamlessly and still have time for social life and leisure. Inevitably, we discover that we cannot do it all.

A life of prayer helps so much at this point. Turning to God and asking for guidance can be life-saving. Learning to be single is difficult when we feel fear, loneliness, anxiety, overwork, and distress of various sorts. But prayer can help bring us face-to-face with deep joy, powerful relationships, and a renewed sense of connection to God and God's creation. Journeying often means walking through difficulties, not around them. With God as our guide, we will reach our goal.

What guidance do you need from God today?

SEEING JESUS

Now on that same day two of them were going to
a village called Emmaus, about seven miles from
Jerusalem, and talking with each other about
all these things that had happened. While they
were talking and discussing, Jesus himself came
near and went with them, but their eyes were
kept from recognizing him.

LUKE 24:13-16

Two people are walking down the road to Emmaus
in this scene, mourning the events of the day. Jesus has been
crucified, and their hope for the redemption of Israel is gone.
They know that Jesus' body is gone, but they do not yet understand the Resurrection.

We are sometimes like these travelers. Through divorce or
death or the end of a relationship, our hopes are dashed and
the one who we thought would bring us to "happily ever
after" is with us no more. We see no resurrection in our
future. Death of one sort or another has won, and new life
seems impossible. Still, we can take a cue from the two walking toward Emmaus. Though their hopes have been shattered, still they invite the stranger to walk with them and to
stay at their home. Jesus accepts, and at the table he takes the

bread, blesses it, and breaks it, and suddenly the two travelers recognize Jesus. They know now that he is risen, that he has opened up new possibilities to them as they walked and ate with him.

It is equally likely we will fail to recognize resurrection and new life when they first appear at our side. But as we welcome whatever appears, perhaps our eyes, too, will be opened and new possibilities made clear. Resurrection is always a surprise.

When has new life or resurrection surprised you?

GATHERING TODAY'S TREASURES

The LORD is my chosen portion and my cup;
> you hold my lot.
The boundary lines have fallen for me in pleasant
> places;
> I have a goodly heritage. . . .
You show me the path of life.
> In your presence there is fullness of joy;
> in your right hand are pleasures forevermore.

PSALM 16:5–6, 11

There is a maxim in computers: a poor manual system for doing something will not be made better simply by computerizing it. The same is true of being single and getting married. Believing that another person, the magical "Right One," will solve all our unhappiness is unlikely to work. If we want to be happily married someday, we must first be comfortable being single.

I have friends who spend their days wishing that this were not so. They spend much of their time and energy wishing for a relationship that will instantly make their worlds wonderful. But I suspect most of them will not be happy with anything they find, because they are first and foremost uncomfortable with themselves. If they land in a relationship that seems perfect, the illusion may hold for a while, but in the end, unresolved emotions and problems simply resurface, and the unhappy person is unhappy again.

God desires good things for each of us and gives us a goodly heritage. God wants to show us the path of life, one in which we will know the fullness of the life we have been given. But we cannot walk that pathway if we are intent on following only our own guidance. God waits, hand outstretched, to show us the great pleasures in our life right now. Gather those treasures first, and wait for what another day will bring later.

> *What illusions or unproductive hopes*
> *prevent you from gathering*
> *today's treasures?*

BECOMING ALL WE ARE MEANT TO BE

> "[The kingdom of heaven] is like a mustard seed,
> which, when sown upon the ground, is the smallest
> of all the seeds on earth; yet when it is sown it grows
> up and becomes the greatest of all shrubs, and puts
> forth large branches, so that the birds of the air can
> make nests in its shade."
>
> MARK 4:31–32

Of all the things I hope to imitate, that little mustard seed is at the top of the list. From the smallest of grains eventually comes a tree that becomes home to others. In each of us lives that wonderful mustard seed, and from each of us can come the tree—big, alive, wonderful, and of service to others.

Single friends sometimes tell me (and I know the feeling myself) that we are somehow incomplete by ourselves. Fairy tales and movies reinforce that notion—we are incomplete until we find "our other half." But the Bible tells us this is not so. That little mustard seed is whole, all by itself, and it holds within it amazing potential. The seed needs dirt, water, and sunshine to help it grow to its full potential. We, too, need support in the form of the love of God and others, but that love can come from so many places besides a life partner. Often we need only choose to absorb the nutrients we need from the world around us, and we can flourish. And by becoming all we were meant to be, we can then offer of ourselves to others. So go ahead, make the choice. Be a mustard seed.

What would make your mustard seed grow?

GETTING ALONG TOGETHER

May the God of steadfastness and encouragement
grant you to live in harmony with one another,
in accordance with Christ Jesus, so that together
you may with one voice glorify the God and Father
of our Lord Jesus Christ.

ROMANS 15:5–6

When I read this passage, I sometimes hear the voice of Rodney King, the African American man whose brutal beating by police officers was captured on videotape. After the police officers were exonerated, riots broke out, and finally in desperation Rodney King appeared on television, pleading in the now famous line: "Can't we all just get along?"

It is a line we in the church need to keep uppermost in our thoughts. If our job is to glorify God and to live like Jesus as best we can, then what does it matter if we are married or single, black or white, gay or straight, male or female, lay or clergy? Why must some groups be normative and others, if not abnormal, not quite comfortable for the church?

The answer to that question, of course, is that we are all still in the process of becoming what God calls us to be. Each of us consciously or unconsciously carries various prejudices and stereotypes. This is an unavoidable human condition.

The times when our preconceived ideas about others meet the reality of a living and breathing person are opportunities for us to learn from one another. They may be difficult moments, sometimes full of anger and hatred, but they are still opportunities. Maybe, with a little divine guidance, some of the hatred can turn to understanding and love.

Someday, perhaps, we will be able to get along and live with fewer separations between us, and we will then be able to turn our voices together and, as one, glorify God.

What prevents you from living in harmony with others?

A PURPOSE IN THE FOG

> I thank my God every time I remember you, con-
> stantly praying with joy in every one of my prayers
> for all of you, because of your sharing in the gospel
> from the first day until now. I am confident of this,
> that the one who began a good work among you will
> bring it to completion by the day of Jesus Christ.
>
> PHILIPPIANS 1:3–6

Does God call some of us to be single? Some be-
lieve singleness is a clear call from God, while others say such
a view harms those who are unhappily single. Most would
agree, however, that it is often difficult to discern one's call
except in hindsight. For a variety of reasons, most adults today will be single for some period of their lives. Some will
find that time easy and enjoyable, while others will suffer and
wish to be married as soon as possible. But for all of us, the
value of those periods of being single can only be fully deter-
mined by looking back at our lives and seeing how those
times fit the overall pattern of an entire lifetime.

In hindsight, some of us will find that we learned valuable
skills while we were single or that we discovered more about
an important aspect of ourselves. Others of us will sense that
we have been single all our lives because we had work to do,

something to accomplish that would have been put aside had we married. But in the midst of the struggle, our view is usually short and foggy. As we would do when driving a car through thick fog, sometimes we have to just keep going, slowly and carefully, watching as best we can, knowing that eventually we will reach our destination and be home.

Are you confident that God began a good work in you and is bringing it to completion?

JOURNEY TOWARD LOVE

"You shall love your neighbor as yourself."

MATTHEW 22:39

Often, when we hear this commandment, we focus on the first part: love your neighbor. But I think that misses the point. "Love your neighbor as yourself" is what we are told. How will we love our neighbor, then, if we do not love ourselves?

On the other hand, sometimes it is the neighbor or the friend who teaches us to love ourselves. I remember some younger days when I did not think much of myself. My sense of self-worth required a great deal of nurturing by friends who cared about me. By listening to me and contradicting my negative statements about myself, they were loving me as they loved themselves. And by doing that, they taught me to love myself so that I, too, could turn around and love others.

Perhaps it is the proverbial chicken-and-egg problem. We begin by loving our neighbor as best we are able. When we are loved in return, we learn a deeper love of ourselves, which enables us to love better in return, and the love spirals outward and spreads. Love is contagious.

What do you love in yourself?

LISTENING TO THE CALL

And when you turn to the right or when you turn to
the left, your ears shall hear a word behind you,
saying, "This is the way; walk in it."

ISAIAH 30:21

We often confuse being alone with being lonely. A call to a single life, however, whether permanent or for a time, need not be a call to a lonely life. Even those who live alone can have a full and active life. Solitude is not a call to loneliness, sadness, or despair.

But there may be things we are called to learn, to experience, to find in a life lived without a partner. Maybe we need to find out who we are alone after many years of living with others. Or perhaps some project has been put on hold for years while we took care of family, and now it is time to complete the task we put aside long ago. Possibly there is some emotion we need to face, something we need to know that we will discover only in a solitary life. We may not even understand why we are called to be single right now. Fortunately, understanding is not necessary at the start. If we listen to the call, living with whatever discomfort it brings, we are likely to discover great riches in the future.

Is there something you need to explore or
do while you are single?

EACH ONE MATTERS

> "Just so, I tell you, there will be more joy in heaven over one sinner who repents than over ninety-nine righteous persons who need no repentance."
>
> LUKE 15:7

Most of the time we think of repentance as simply being sorry for something we've done, but its fuller meaning involves turning around, seeing things in a new way. Perhaps, for some of us, repentance involves giving up our anger at God for "inflicting" our present lives—including work, friends, single status, or whatever—on us, and looking at our lives in a whole new way.

For me, seeing a new way was a gradual process that took many years to complete. Repentance was a process of turning around and experiencing gratitude to God for the blessings in my life, rather than reacting with anger or grudging acceptance for the burdens. An amazing peace accompanied that new way of seeing, and I experience a deep sense of quiet and joy about my life as it is now. All of which makes it not so hard to imagine that there is, indeed, great joy in heaven when even one of us manages to turn around.

Do you need to turn around to see the blessings in your life?

NO INSTANT SOLUTIONS

> Jesus, full of the Holy Spirit, returned from the
> Jordan and was led by the Spirit in the wilderness,
> where for forty days he was tempted by the devil.
>
> LUKE 4:1–2

This has to be one of the ultimate "wandering in the desert" stories. Jesus roams the desert for forty days, and at the end of this time he is famished. The devil approaches him and offers him bread and power and authority, but Jesus turns it all down. It is not what he really needs.

Sometimes I feel like Jesus wandering in the desert. At the moments when I am most tired, I am assaulted by media and cultural messages that tout being a couple. Ads and commercials tell me that if I just wear or own this or that product, the "Right One" will magically appear. Songs on the radio feature people singing that the love of their life has either just appeared or just left. Everything that surrounds me tells me I should be thinking about finding a partner, but that is a message that comes from outside me, not from within.

It is not that I shy away from community or even from romance, if it happens to appear in my life. But I'm not afraid of solitude and silence either, and there are definitely times when I envy Jesus his forty days of peace and quiet in the desert. Sometimes, as with Jesus, those periods of wandering alone leave us hungry for something, but not for what Satan has to offer. Our souls long for what God provides in our lives. Finding a partner, any old one, will not make me happy. Neither will buying a new perfume or a new shirt or a new car. There is nothing wrong with any of these things, but they are momentary satisfactions, not the deep ones for which our souls long. It is easy enough to be tempted by the bread, power, and authority that Satan offers Jesus, but these things will not actually lead us to God and a soul-filled life. Instant solutions, things that sound too good to be true, are usually just that. Listen deeper within you, to God's voice, not the commercial that promises you success on sale.

What do you really need?

PLANTED WHERE WE BELONG

Then he said to me, "Mortal, these bones are the whole house of Israel. They say, 'Our bones are dried up, and our hope is lost; we are cut off completely.' Therefore prophesy, and say to them, Thus says the Lord GOD: I am going to open your graves, and bring you up from your graves, O my people; and I will bring you back to the land of Israel. And you shall know that I am the LORD, when I open your graves, and bring you up from your graves, O my people. I will put my spirit within you, and you shall live, and I will place you on your own soil."

EZEKIEL 37:11–14

Many of us who are single today are single again. Having lost a spouse to divorce or death, some feel like these bones in Ezekiel: "Our bones are dried up, and our hope is lost; we are cut off completely." For many, being single again was never part of the plan. Dealing with the changes in identity, finding new social spaces that are comfortable, and living alone are challenges, not joys.

But God promises to breathe new life into us if we are willing. Ezekiel promises us that we will know God's presence when we are brought out of our graves, when we are planted in our own soil. I am fond of the promise that we will be planted in our own soil. It implies that God has a unique place in mind for each of us—a place in which we, individually, will thrive and know God. We may feel like a dried seed at this moment. We may be dry bones, but God will plant us where we belong and bring us new life, flesh, and spirit, and we will be on our feet once again.

What do you think of the promise of being planted in your own soil?

CHAPTER FOUR
MANNA IN THE WILDERNESS

ACCEPTING AND BEING MANNA

And Moses said to Aaron, "Take a jar, and put an omer of manna in it, and place it before the LORD, to be kept throughout your generations." As the LORD commanded Moses, so Aaron placed it before the covenant, for safekeeping. The Israelites ate manna forty years, until they came to a habitable land; they ate manna, until they came to the border of the land of Canaan.

EXODUS 16:33–35

Food was sometimes scarce for the Israelites as they wandered in the desert. Being nomads during this time, they could not stop to plant or provide for themselves. Therefore they turned to Moses, begging him to ask God for help, and God provided for them. Daily they were given manna, enough to sustain them until the next day.

So it is, too, in our lives. We can't, as individuals, take care of every one of our own needs. We always need help—from God, from friends and family, from colleagues, and from others. When we try to do everything by ourselves, in fact, we often burn out and miss much of the richness of life. God did not intend for us to operate independently of one another. The sum of all of us together is more magnificent, more wonderful, than any of the individual parts.

We, like the Israelites, can be grateful for the manna in our wilderness—for the people who day by day care, offer support and encouragement, and teach us how to live a rich, full life. We can be manna for others as well. Accepting manna and being manna for others are gifts of God to us and to each other. Partake of it and share it freely.

What manna do you need, and what manna have you to share?

ROLE MODELS IN OUR MIDST

Where there is no vision, the people perish.

PROVERBS 29:18 (KJV)

*S*ometimes I meet people who keep themselves so busy they can hardly see straight. Though I am no stranger to a busy life, these people seem to manufacture busy lives in order to avoid being by themselves. Their lives look more frantic than full, and I wonder if they have any vision of the possibility of living singly and contentedly.

There have been so few models of a joyful single life held up for most of us that it is no wonder that many have no vision to sustain them. If we had single relatives, they were pitied, not admired. A single uncle as a "bachelor" was not quite as pitiful as a maiden, or "spinster," aunt, but neither of them was a model our parents encouraged us to follow. Many of us who are single grew up without any positive visions or associations for a life lived without a partner.

Today, however, with such a large percentage of the population being single, there are models and visions all around us. A friend of mine, whose wife died recently, asked me what I like about being single, and I told him about the things I love—the freedoms I have and the ability to shape my own life. He glimpsed a new vision of the single life that day and found much in it that appealed to him. Without a vision, Proverbs tells us, we will perish. But there are people all around us who can help guide us to that vision. Listen to the prophets in your midst.

Who might guide you to a new vision
of the single life?

TOUCH

And all in the crowd were trying to touch him, for
power came out from him and healed all of them.

LUKE 6:19

I have a prayer corner in my home, a place reserved
for my time with God. In it I keep my favorite prayer books,
some candles, my rosary, and other helps to my prayer life.
One of the things in it that I like best is a very simple statue of
a person kneeling, almost leaning, against the legs and knees
of Jesus. Jesus' hands lovingly rest on the person's head, and it
is clear that healing is taking place. Sometimes I stare long-
ingly at that statue and notice how much I miss simple touch.
Not sex, as our culture would have us focus on, but touch
itself. Jesus often healed people by touching them. It was a
healing, life-giving gift. And there are days when I wish to be
the person kneeling against Jesus with his hands resting on
my head.

When I find myself really missing human contact, sometimes I schedule a massage for myself, not to work out sore
muscles, but to enjoy the sense of being touched. My skin
seems to hunger for the physical presence of other human
beings, for the reassurance and the healing that contact
brings. I treasure, too, those friends of mine who are "huggers,"

who know that touch matters, particularly in the lives of single people. The best gifts come from friends who are not afraid to wrap me in their arms and hold me tight for a moment. Their touch brings great healing to my soul.

What do you do when you need the healing touch of others?

SUPPORT GROUPS

First, I thank my God through Jesus Christ for all
of you, because your faith is proclaimed throughout
the world. For God, whom I serve with my spirit by
announcing the gospel of his Son, is my witness
that without ceasing I remember you always in my
prayers, asking that by God's will I may somehow
at last succeed in coming to you. For I am longing
to see you so that I may share with you some spiritual
gift to strengthen you—or rather so that we may
be mutually encouraged by each other's faith, both
yours and mine.

ROMANS 1:8–12

Living alone means that I do not always have someone handy with whom to talk things over. Many times I've come home from work or from another activity with something on my mind and picked up the phone to call a friend. But one of the best things I've had in my life is a prayer group that offered me regular support and encouragement. We met once a month and kept up with each other between those times. I looked forward to those evenings each month when we would pray together, share our hopes and concerns, and offer each other encouragement and support.

Most of us can benefit from this kind of help, from a close group of people who offer support and prayers. Some of us need the encouragement of others who have traveled our particular road already—people who have survived divorce or the death of a beloved spouse. Or perhaps we just need a supportive community in general. My own group consisted of women who simply came together to listen to one another and pray.

Churches and various community organizations offer all sorts of support groups. If you can't find one you like, put together your own. Invite some like-minded friends to covenant with you for a period of time and experiment with the kind of prayer and encouragement you can offer one another. Being part of a community of people who care that we are well and safe and happy can make all the difference in the quality of our lives.

What kind of support group might be helpful in your life?

ASKING FOR HELP

My God, my God, why have you forsaken me?
> Why are you so far from helping me, from the
> words of my groaning?
O my God, I cry by day, but you do not answer;
> and by night, but find no rest. . . .
Yet it was you who took me from the womb;
> you kept me safe on my mother's breast.
On you I was cast from my birth,
> and since my mother bore me you have been my
> God.
Do not be far from me,
> for trouble is near
> and there is no one to help.

PSALM 22:1–2, 9–11

It is easy, particularly when we live alone, to feel that there is no one to help when we are in trouble. We don't want to pick up the phone and "bother" someone when we are sick and in need of assistance. We feel lonely late at night, but it seems too late to call anyone. So we suffer by ourselves, adding self-pity to whatever ails us in the first place.

I remember one time when I spent the night worried and scared because I was having difficulty breathing. The next morning I made an appointment to see my doctor, but I was too sick to drive and had to ask my friend and next-door neighbor to take me. She was furious that I hadn't called her for help during the night. I will never forget her standing in my yard in tears, angry and hurt that I didn't ask for help when I'd needed it. Never again did I hesitate to ask her for assistance.

So often it is easy to just feel sorry for ourselves or believe that it is a weakness to ask for help. We sit alone and wonder why God has forsaken us. But God is right next door or a phone call away, in the form of a neighbor or a friend who would gladly lend a hand or an ear if only we summon the courage to ask.

What makes it so hard to ask others for help?

NURTURING COMMUNITIES

When it grew late, his disciples came to him and said,
"This is a deserted place, and the hour is now very
late; send them away so that they may go into the
surrounding country and villages and buy something
for themselves to eat." But he answered them, "You
give them something to eat." They said to him,
"Are we to go and buy two hundred denarii worth
of bread, and give it to them to eat?" And he said
to them, "How many loaves have you? Go and see."
When they had found out, they said, "Five, and
two fish." Then he ordered them to get all the people
to sit down in groups on the green grass. So they
sat down in groups of hundreds and of fifties. Taking
the five loaves and the two fish, he looked up to
heaven, and blessed and broke the loaves, and gave
them to his disciples to set before the people; and
he divided the two fish among them all. And all ate
and were filled.

MARK 6:35–42

With our culture's focus on couples and families,
sometimes I forget that nurturing comes from other groups
as well. In Mark's description of the feeding of the five thousand, Jesus tells people to sit down in groups of hundreds and

fifties. He does not send the people out to find food for themselves, as the disciples suggest, nor does he tell them to sit down in family groups. Jesus has them sit down with others who are around them, and in these groups of hundreds and fifties, people eat as much as they want and have food left over.

There are many places today, too, where we can be filled to overflowing. These do not need to be family units. I find wonderful support from some of my colleagues at work, and many have become friends on whom I can rely. Friends and groups online feed me as well, and the bytes on my computer screen bring me laughter, encouragement, and help. Even temporary communities—people gathered for a retreat or a pilgrimage —become a source of nourishment in my life. For the hours or days that we share together, we offer one another sustenance for body and soul. We can be part of all sorts of communities. There are groups of hundreds and fifties all around.

Does anything prevent you from finding a support group?

> While he was still speaking to the crowds, his mother
> and his brothers were standing outside, wanting
> to speak to him. Someone told him, "Look, your
> mother and your brothers are standing outside,
> wanting to speak to you." But to the one who had
> told him this, Jesus replied, "Who is my mother,
> and who are my brothers?" And pointing to his
> disciples, he said, "Here are my mother and my
> brothers! For whoever does the will of my Father
> in heaven is my brother and sister and mother."
>
> MATTHEW 12:46–50

I think Jesus was way ahead of his time with this declaration. Two thousand years ago, he redefined family in a way that has come alive quite vividly in the 1990s. Given our mobile society, few of us live near our biological family anymore, and many are creating new "families" for themselves.

But Jesus said it first. He didn't worry about the blood ties that attached him to what people considered his family; instead he declared that all who follow the will of God were his brothers, sisters, and mother. Jesus redefined the family, and many of us need to do that too. The church can become a new family for us, a place where we are known and welcome.

Others, living alone but wanting to be around children, befriend families in their neighborhood or church, spending time with the children and giving the parent or parents needed respite from child care. There are many ways to form family for those of us who don't live in family units or have our own family close by. Being single doesn't mean that we don't have lots of love to share with others. Following the will of God may mean, as it did for Jesus, that we create family for ourselves.

Where do you find "family" in your world?

For this reason, since the day we heard it, we have not
ceased praying for you and asking that you may be
filled with the knowledge of God's will in all spiritual
wisdom and understanding, so that you may lead
lives worthy of the Lord, fully pleasing to him, as you
bear fruit in every good work and as you grow in the
knowledge of God.

COLOSSIANS 1:9–10

A friend of mine was so lonely once that he spent
hours and hours online in chat rooms from early in the
morning until late at night in order to feel a connection to
someone. It overwhelmed his life and his pocketbook. This
is not to say that computer chat rooms are bad, but anything
that occupies so much of our time, to the exclusion of God
and those around us, hampers our growth and our ability to
be what God intends for us.

If we are not growing in strength and patience and joy,
turning to fantasy rarely solves the problem. Turning to God
is needed, but we may require help to do that. A spiritual director, a trusted pastor, or a trained counselor may be able to
help us uncover the source of our misery and grow in the
knowledge of God. Close friends can help us by praying with

us that we "may be filled with the knowledge of God's will in all spiritual wisdom and understanding" (Col 1:9). Though many of us will endure natural periods of grieving, God does not ultimately will us to be miserable. Many people around us can help and support us. They can teach us about or model a full life, one that is pleasing to God (and to us!) and that bears good fruit in its many works.

Who can help you grow in the knowledge of God?

FRIENDS

> After this Paul left Athens and went to Corinth. There
> he found a Jew named Aquila, a native of Pontus, who
> had recently come from Italy with his wife Priscilla,
> because Claudius had ordered all Jews to leave Rome.
> Paul went to see them, and, because he was of the
> same trade, he stayed with them, and they worked
> together—by trade they were tentmakers.
>
> ACTS 18:1–3

Friendships matter immensely in the lives of singles, not only friendships with other single people, but also friendships with those who are married. Paul often refers to Aquila and Priscilla in the New Testament: several times in Acts, then in 1 Corinthians, Romans, and Titus. He stays with them, travels with them, and sends his greetings through others when they are apart. Obviously, friends matter a great deal to Paul.

We need friends of all sorts in our lives. If, for instance, we have only single friends, then our perspective is limited. We see only what we know, and our worldview becomes small and narrow. We need friends of the same sex and friends of the opposite sex, friends who are married as well as friends who are single. We need friends of all different sorts if we are to meet God in all God's guises, for God lives within each one of us.

How diverse are your friends?

E-MAIL

Paul, called to be an apostle of Christ Jesus by
the will of God, and our brother Sosthenes,

To the church of God that is in Corinth, to those
who are sanctified in Christ Jesus, called to be
saints, together with all those who in every place
call on the name of our Lord Jesus Christ, both
their Lord and ours:

Grace to you and peace from God our Father and
the Lord Jesus Christ.

1 CORINTHIANS 1:1–3

Given the number of Paul's letters that made it into the Bible, can you imagine how many he would have written if he'd had E-mail? He probably would have been one of the world's most prolific writers.

E-mail has been such a wonderful addition to my life in the last few years. As I move around the country, traveling for business or personal reasons, I meet people I don't want to lose track of, and E-mail prevents that from happening. I come home from work at the end of the day and usually log on to see what's up in the world. Most evenings there are notes from friends, and I enjoy reading about what is going on in their lives and writing back about my own adventures.

E-mail is one way I stay connected to the world, to friends who live out of the area.

A lot of what we know about Paul's ministry comes from the letters he left behind. In those letters we read about his love for the people of God, of his concern for friends. His deep pastoral care for those he has met is always obvious. And though I am not Paul, I hope my own E-mail is a little like that too. Notes from friends and my answers in response are a ministry going on over the phone wires, and both the care and concern I receive and the love I try to pass back in bytes and bites fill my soul. During the best days and the worst moments, they are a lifeline, a way of being connected to God's good people.

How do you keep in touch with friends?

PETS

> And God said, "Let the waters bring forth swarms
> of living creatures, and let birds fly above the
> earth across the dome of the sky." So God created
> the great sea monsters and every living creature
> that moves, of every kind, with which the waters
> swarm, and every winged bird of every kind. And
> God saw that it was good.
>
> GENESIS 1:20–21

When I say that I live alone, I am actually misstating the facts. I live with a cat, or from his perspective, he allows me to live with him. Anyone who lives with a cat knows better than to say that they "own" a cat—cats clearly own us. I learned long ago that when Codi wants something at four in the morning, it is easier to get up and meet the need than it is to try to continue sleeping. He is one of the best guards I have against getting too set in my own ways.

Still, I can't imagine living without him. Cats, and dogs too, have this uncanny ability to care for us. Codi's method of attacking and wrestling his catnip toy to the ground keeps me laughing, but he also knows when I am sad and in need of a cuddle. Sensing my mood, he crawls up on my lap and makes himself at home, a warm and comforting presence.

A friend of mine, more the dog sort of person, loves to take his dog to the park and watch him run. He meets all sorts of other people there with their dogs and enjoys the social time as well as his pet.

God must have thought that the animals would be good for us as well, for in Genesis 2, before God makes Eve, God gives Adam the animals to name. They turn out not to be quite the partner God had in mind for Adam, but I'll bet they were still wonderful companions. God made all of us—people and animals—and found us good. It seems only fitting, then, that we should delight in one another's company.

Does or would a pet make a difference in your life?

LIFE-SAVING MEDICINE

Faithful friends are a sturdy shelter:
   whoever finds one has found a treasure.
Faithful friends are beyond price;
   no amount can balance their worth.
Faithful friends are life-saving medicine;
   and those who fear the Lord will find them.

SIRACH 6:14-16

Friends, as Sirach says, are life-saving medicine. Friends who can be with us in our joys and our difficulties are essential in the life of singles, particularly those who live alone. None of us is made to live in isolation from the world; we are meant to love others and to be loved as well.

Just recently I relearned the lesson about the importance of friendship. I moved across the country for a new job. Moving a whole household is a big chore. When I made the decision to move, a friend who lived where I was moving called and offered to help me unpack. Though I gave her ample opportunity to get out of her promise, she insisted on coming and helping me put everything away. My belongings were completely unpacked (even the pictures were hung) within two days. That kind gesture went a long way toward making me feel at home in strange surroundings.

Another friend of mine needed time away from her high-stress job and arranged a month's leave. She lived a couple of states away from me and needed a real break from her situation. So she came and stayed with me for a month, and we took the opportunity to do all the tourist things I'd never done: see plays, shop, and have nice dinners out. Being able to provide a place of refuge for a month was a gift I could give her, but I got so much companionship and pleasure in return. As Sirach says, "Faithful friends are beyond price" (Sir 6:15).

> *How have you and your friends been*
> *life-saving medicine to one another?*

GOD PROVIDES

But Moses said to the LORD, "O my Lord, I have never
been eloquent, neither in the past nor even now that
you have spoken to your servant; but I am slow of
speech and slow of tongue." Then the LORD said to
him, "Who gives speech to mortals?… Is it not I, the
LORD? Now go, and I will be with your mouth and
teach you what you are to speak." But he said, "O
my Lord, please send someone else." Then the anger
of the LORD was kindled against Moses and he said,
"What of your brother Aaron, the Levite? I know that
he can speak fluently….You shall speak to him and
put the words in his mouth; and I will be with your
mouth and with his mouth, and will teach you what
you shall do."

EXODUS 4:10–15

This must have been a pretty wild day for Moses.
He finds this bush burning in the desert, and the voice of
God tells him to go into Egypt and free the Israelites from
Pharaoh. "Please send someone else," Moses tells God. "I am
slow of speech and slow of tongue" (not to mention that
Moses has his father-in-law's flock to tend and probably quite
a few other things on his to-do list). But God has other plans:
Aaron will help Moses do what needs to be done.

Help often comes from unexpected sources like that. This last Christmas my work had me traveling constantly from mid-November until mid-December, with only brief trips home in between. I seriously considered skipping the Christmas tree and holiday decorations. Time was tight, and I wouldn't be home to enjoy them much anyway. But during the first week of December the management office of the apartment complex I live in announced that it was "customer appreciation week," which meant, among other things, that you could buy a tree through them and they would bring it to your apartment and put it in your tree stand for you. I came home from a trip one night to a beautiful tree, all installed and lights strung.

Just when we think we cannot do anything more, help comes from unexpected quarters. Someone puts up our Christmas tree for us or speaks for us or provides assistance in another way. Through the kindness of friends, families, strangers, and apartment-complex managers, God does provide.

Where has unexpected help come from in your life?

NO CLONES

Indeed, the body does not consist of one member but of many. If the foot would say, "Because I am not a hand, I do not belong to the body," that would not make it any less a part of the body. And if the ear would say, "Because I am not an eye, I do not belong to the body," that would not make it any less a part of the body. If the whole body were an eye, where would the hearing be? If the whole body were hearing, where would the sense of smell be? But as it is, God arranged the members in the body, each one of them, as he chose. If all were a single member, where would the body be? As it is, there are many members, yet one body.

1 CORINTHIANS 12:14–20

This often-quoted passage from 1 Corinthians reminds us that we do not have to be clones of one another to be one body in Christ. We belong to God and to one another, but that does not mean that we must all be alike, that we must have the same function. A body composed of only one element of any of us makes no sense. Of what use would a body be if it were composed only of ears or only of eyes?

In the same way, a society composed of clones would be limited and uninteresting—the kind of nightmare society painted in some science-fiction novels. Each of us brings a unique perspective to the whole. We enrich one another by having and sharing our different perspectives. I have a married friend who enjoys getting away with her single friends simply because she feels claustrophobic when her whole world centers on people who are married with children. She needs to feel the more solitary part of herself, and she can do that with others who understand that experience. In the same way, she brings her life in community to those of us who live alone. We are both enriched by the conversation. We are many members with different perspectives, none of them innately right or wrong. We are many members, but one body.

How does diversity spice up your life?

GOD AS MANNA

The whole congregation of the Israelites complained
against Moses and Aaron in the wilderness. The
Israelites said to them, "If only we had died by the
hand of the LORD in the land of Egypt, when we
sat by the fleshpots and ate our fill of bread; for you
have brought us out into this wilderness to kill this
whole assembly with hunger."

EXODUS 16:2-3

Many of us have been surprised by life. We
have been pulled into the desert, away from the life we were
expecting or once knew, and we are asked to wander for an
unspecified period of time before we come to something we
can call home. Not a few of us have probably felt like the
Israelites complaining that Moses brought them into the
desert only to suffer.

This is the third time that the Israelites complain to
Moses. First they feared the Egyptians in pursuit of them.
Then they had no water to drink, and now they are without
food. Each time the people complain, Moses turns to God,
and God provides what is needed. I think God does that for
us, too, though probably less dramatically than in Exodus.
When I feel despondent or lonely in the desert, God appears

in the love of friends who write or call or visit. God also exists in my cat, who seems to know when climbing on my lap or curling up for a snuggle is needed. Sometimes, when God is feeling really sneaky, he provides help through a good laugh from a joke posted online that makes me lighten up a little and sense the divine. God appears in more ways than we will ever know or be able to count.

In what ways has God appeared in your life?

CHAPTER FIVE
BY THE WATERS OF BABYLON

LIVING IN BABYLON

By the rivers of Babylon—
　　there we sat down and there we wept
　　when we remembered Zion.
On the willows there
　　we hung up our harps.
For there our captors
　　asked us for songs,
and our tormentors asked for mirth, saying,
　　"Sing us one of the songs of Zion!"

PSALM 137:1-3

I f one more person asks me what "a nice girl like you is doing still single," I just might scream loud enough for you to hear it, wherever you are. Questions like that, though complimentary at one level, leave me feeling like I've been exiled from Zion and am living in Babylon.

Sometimes it seems as if all the media—television, radio, newspapers, magazines, and ads everywhere—focus on romance and togetherness, as if this were the most important thing in the whole wide world. Singles on television shows spend a lot of energy trying to find romance or bemoaning the fact that they haven't. Country-and-western songs are the classics, of course, in moaning about lost love. And advertising agencies use sex to sell everything from toothpaste to cars. "Sing us one of the songs of Zion," it all seems to say. "Sing us one of the songs about the love you don't have."

Now, I've got nothing against love and romance; they can be quite wonderful. But there are so many other facets to my life that are equally valuable. I love my work, my many dear friends, and my life as a whole. I don't feel the need to focus on what isn't a part of my life right now. Why must others?

What are the popular images that make it hard for you to be single in a couples' world?

GOD IN THE DARK

The light shines in the darkness, and the darkness did not overcome it.

JOHN 1:5

There are times in my life when nights are difficult for me. The workday is over, the evening activities have ended, I am alone in my bed, and occasionally fear, loneliness, or sadness sets in. This is particularly true when I am overly tired or stressed, when I am working too hard and not playing enough. It is easy to keep those feelings at bay while I am busy or while people are around. But sometimes late at night the feelings come unbidden and unwelcome, and I wonder if God knows or cares.

The darkness of the night also used to frighten me. I felt completely alone in the black of night, so I warded off the feelings of fear with night-lights and hall lights or whatever else was needed. I wanted nothing more than to have someone to lie with, someone to keep me safe. That fear of the dark was really a fear of the darkness inside me, of my own unresolved issues, and night-lights were only a placebo. As I began to confront the darkness inside me and as my relationship with God deepened, my fear of the night faded away. All alone in the dark I finally discovered that God is with me in the night, as in the light, and wrapped in God's presence, the nighttime began to feel like a warm and comfortable quilt. By befriending the darkness within and without, I found a new and welcome friend, a friend who brought gifts I'd never imagined.

Is there darkness or loneliness inside you
that needs to be brought into the light?

SPOUSE STEALING

> You shall not covet your neighbor's house; you shall
> not covet your neighbor's wife, or male or female
> slave, or ox, or donkey, or anything that belongs to
> your neighbor.
>
> EXODUS 20:17

One of the things I most dislike about being single is the reaction I get from married people who think I am trying to steal their spouse. They respond to me, and other singles, this way not because of anything we have done. We haven't been caught in any sort of tryst with their spouse. We haven't even been caught flirting. They believe we are after their husband or wife because we are single, and being single means we must be miserable and willing to do anything—including stealing their spouse.

I remember visiting a friend one Christmas and spending the day with her husband's large family. All the adults in the room were married except for me. Because I live in the business world, I was in the living room talking business with the men, and it was clear this distressed the women. Every effort was made to bring me into the kitchen with the rest of the women, away from the husbands. Recently a male friend told me this same kind of story from the other point of view. The wives of his married male friends often guard the time their husbands spend with him, because they are afraid their husbands might find his single lifestyle more appealing than their marriages.

Well, I do not covet my neighbor's spouse, but convincing people of that can be difficult work. Some married friends seem to feel that it is not possible to be happy as a single person and that stealing away someone else's spouse is preferable to being single. Why can't they see that their unfounded suspicion is very painful to me?

Why is it hard for others to imagine that you might really enjoy your single existence?

ANGER AS A BUILDING BLOCK

Let no evil talk come out of your mouths, but only
what is useful for building up, as there is need, so
that your words may give grace to those who hear.

EPHESIANS 4:29

Something that annoys me is the assumption that I have no life because I am single. People tend to think that I have no obligations and that I suffer less when something goes wrong or there is too much work to do. Obviously—to them—any commitments I might have are less important than their own family engagements and responsibilities. I am willing to help cover for their family emergencies or put in my share of overtime, but when it gets excessive I quickly become angry. I find my anger rising, as well, when I hear about those who are paid less than married colleagues simply because they are single.

So I like this passage from Ephesians, which tells me to let no evil talk come from my mouth unless it is useful for building up a situation. It tells me that it is fair for me to be angry when others take advantage of me. It is appropriate for me to work toward developing a workplace where my life and needs are respected in the same ways as those with spouses and children. In a workplace where we all try to accommodate each other's needs, where we value each person's life circumstances equally, grace abounds.

How can you use your anger to build a better world?

PAIRS AND SPARES

Contend, O LORD, with those who contend with me;
    fight against those who fight against me! . . .
For without cause they hid their net for me;
    without cause they dug a pit for my life.
Let ruin come on them unawares.
And let the net that they hid ensnare them;
    let them fall in it—to their ruin.

PSALM 35:1, 7–8

I am easily angered by people who look askance at me for being single. I remember once when someone suggested that the young adult fellowship group in my church should be called "Pairs and Spares." Very coldly, I replied that I was not a spare. At that moment, I felt like the psalmist. I wished for ruin to "come on them unawares."

In retrospect, I know that the person who suggested the name meant no harm. The name has a cute sound to it. It rhymes, and people like rhymes. Despite how harmful I found the name, I think the person actually meant it to be inclusive. It is a title that includes singles and couples. Nonetheless, it is a name often used for fellowship groups in churches, and it hurts. It leaves me feeling like a spare tire in the trunk of a car, something useful only in emergencies.

How can I be a part of a group with that name and still feel good about myself?

Spares, of course, are useful things to have. Who doesn't want a spare lightbulb handy when they need it? But objects, not people, are spares. I am not waiting for anyone's destruction before I become welcome or useful. I am not a spare. I am an individual, one of God's beloved.

How do you respond to being thought of as a spare?

TWO BY TWO IN THE ARK

And God said to Noah, "... Make yourself an ark
of cypress wood; make rooms in the ark, and cover
it inside and out with pitch. . . . For my part, I am
going to bring a flood of waters on the earth, to
destroy from under heaven all flesh in which is the
breath of life.... But I will establish my covenant with
you; and you shall come into the ark, you, your sons,
your wife, and your sons' wives with you. And of
every living thing, of all flesh, you shall bring two of
every kind into the ark, to keep them alive with you."

GENESIS 6:13–14, 17–19

At times it feels like the ark's boarding plan is a
metaphor for the church. We are welcome two by two, rather
than singly. The church understands what to offer a family. It
is a little uncomfortable with us singles. A single friend of
mine, for instance, was very surprised that the church thought
of her differently once she announced her engagement.
Immediately following her announcement, she and her fiancé
received all sorts of invitations to join fellowship groups and
become more involved in church life, even though they had
attended that church for many years. The opposite has been
true for friends who have found themselves newly single and
suddenly not quite as welcome in their old church circles.

Now, I know that Noah needed a male and female of each kind in order to insure the continuation of all species. Even so, the church reproduces through the work of the Spirit, not the flesh. Wanting us to come to church two by two doesn't seem all that necessary.

As a single person, what have been your experiences with the church?

SEPARATE AT CHURCH

> For as in one body we have many members, and not
> all the members have the same function, so we, who
> are many, are one body in Christ, and individually we
> are members one of another.
>
> ROMANS 12:4–5

If we are all members of one another, I wonder why the church works so hard on programming that keeps us separate. Why do we need so many activities at church that are only for couples, for children, for families, for singles?

Many years ago I was a part of a fellowship group for young adults in the church, a group composed of people in their twenties and thirties. As the group aged, the governing board of the church decided that the group should split into two groups: one for couples and one for singles. Rarely have I felt as alienated as I did when told that I was no longer welcome in fellowship with the people I'd been with for many years.

In a time when most families no longer include both children and grandparents, singles and couples, where can we learn about one another? Where can children see the variety of options that will be open to them as adults? Today we learn what it is to be young or old, single or married, not from one another, but from books or the media. The church has a wonderful opportunity to present programs for the whole of the church, to give all of us a place to be with and learn from one another. There is certainly a place for activities that meet the needs of specific groups, but I wish the balance between dividing the people of God and bringing us together were tipped in favor of the latter.

What kind of activities would nourish you at church?

SHARING THE CHORES

I lift up my eyes to the hills—
  from where will my help come?
My help comes from the LORD,
  who made heaven and earth.

PSALM 121:1–2

I love many things about being single, but some things are vexing. One trying thing is not having someone with whom to share the chores.

Recently a friend went with me to the Department of Motor Vehicles to lend moral support in a long struggle to get my car registered. It had been four months of paperwork and frustration caught between the DMVs of three states, and I was at my wit's end. We finally got the car registered, and on the way home she commented that she was grateful for a spouse who could take over when she reached the end of her rope. I would have given anything, about two months into the DMV nightmare, to have had someone else to help me jump through the bureaucratic hoops.

We can, of course, ask for help. But often it is up to us to navigate the day-to-day tasks that must be done. If a child is sick, we are the ones who have to stay home and be caretaker. If the plumbing is broken, we miss a day of work and wait for the plumber. If we live alone or are the sole adult in a household, we are the ones who must take care of the matters of daily living. I know that, in the end, my help comes from God, but my sense is that God worries most about the really big issues in my life, not about the grocery shopping. And there are days when I would be delighted if God felt like taking the cat to the vet or unclogging the bathroom drain for me.

If you could get God to do one chore for you today, what would it be?

PRINCE CHARMING

For God alone my soul waits in silence,
    for my hope is from him.
He alone is my rock and my salvation,
    my fortress; I shall not be shaken.
On God rests my deliverance and my honor;
    my mighty rock, my refuge is in God.

PSALM 62:5–7

When I was younger I dreamed of a Prince Charming who would be my rock and my deliverance. He would swoop down, sweep me off my feet, and carry me away, and we would live happily ever after.

Many of us grew up with that dream of the "Right One," but as we grew older we learned that the world doesn't always operate that way. The fairy tales we learned as children are just that—fairy tales. Some of us fell in love, married, and discovered that the "Right One" wasn't the person for us after all. Others lost someone they loved to death. And some of us never found anyone who seemed destined for us. We all found (even those who are happily married) that no human being can be our mighty rock and redeemer. It is too much to ask of another person. It is too much to ask of ourselves.

I struggled hard with giving up the dream that someone would come along and make my life wonderful. I dated lots of people whom I tried to make into the "Right One." Sometimes I still miss the deep physical comfort that comes from being wrapped in a lover's arms, feeling held and secure. But over time, I came to understand that only God can really be Prince Charming in my life. Only God can be the rock that is immovable, solid, dependable, and always there for me. God fills my life and makes it rich. In that knowledge I find great peace.

How is God your rock and your refuge?

JOB'S UNHELPFUL FRIENDS

Then Zophar the Naamathite answered:
"Should a multitude of words go unanswered,
    and should one full of talk be vindicated?
Should your babble put others to silence,
    and when you mock, shall no one shame you?
For you say, 'My conduct is pure,
    and I am clean in God's sight.'
But oh, that God would speak,
    and open his lips to you,
and that he would tell you the secrets of wisdom!
    For wisdom is many-sided.
Know then that God exacts of you less than your
    guilt deserves.

JOB 11:1–6

Zophar the Naamathite, supposedly a friend of
Job's, is trying to convince Job that he did something to earn
the wrath of God. Job's misdeeds are the reason that God is
making Job suffer, says Zophar. Job must not recognize, or
admit, how awful he has really been.

Zophar meant well with this comment, but as we discover
at the end of the book of Job, he was quite wrong. Zophar assumed a knowledge of God that Zophar did not actually
have, and that is sometimes true of our well-meaning friends

today. Friends and our culture's media messages tell us in a variety of ways that we can avoid pain. Books abound giving advice on being married within a year's time. Friends and advertisements promise us that if we just lost a little weight, acted a little different, wore the right clothes, and so on, our "problems" would be solved. Those friends and messages are about as helpful as Job's three friends were. In the end God made it clear that Job's friends were wrong, and he forced them to make amends to Job.

When we hear these kinds of messages from those around us, we can be confident that they, too, are wrong. We may not understand our circumstances any more than Job could. But we can be confident that we are God's beloved and that God did not "inflict" the single life on us because we are bad people.

Do you really believe that being single is not a punishment from God?

CHAPTER SIX
SEEING A NEW WAY

VIEWED FROM A DIFFERENT ANGLE

Now there was a Pharisee named Nicodemus, a leader
of the Jews. He came to Jesus by night and said to him,
"Rabbi, we know that you are a teacher who has come
from God; for no one can do these signs that you do
apart from the presence of God." Jesus answered him,
"Very truly, I tell you, no one can see the kingdom of
God without being born from above." Nicodemus said
to him, "How can anyone be born after having grown
old? Can one enter a second time into the mother's
womb and be born?" Jesus answered, "Very truly, I tell
you, no one can enter the kingdom of God without
being born of water and Spirit. What is born of the
flesh is flesh, and what is born of the Spirit is spirit. . . ."
Nicodemus said to him, "How can these things be?"
Jesus answered him, "Are you a teacher of Israel, and
yet you do not understand these things?"

JOHN 3:1–6, 9–10

Sometimes the hardest thing in the world is turning something upside down or inside out or sideways to see it
from a new angle. Yet when something doesn't work well,
doesn't look or sound right, that is exactly what we need to
do. Like Nicodemus, we have to struggle with what we have
always known and refashion it.

Though more mundane than Jesus' challenge to Nicodemus, Valentine's Day might be a big opportunity to do just that. The annual festival for people with sweethearts is often very taxing on those who are not in a relationship. We can get our holidays confused and become very Scrooge-like for Valentine's Day, or we can reimage it for ourselves. Perhaps this is a time to remember those we love at this time of year—parents, friends, and neighbors. It is easy to let our lives go speeding by quickly and forget to ever tell these dear people what they mean to us. Valentine's Day can be a time to send a card or an E-mail, make a phone call, and celebrate the love we receive from others. It might also provide an opportunity to remember those whom we have loved and lost. Perhaps it is even a time to love ourselves and buy ourselves flowers or chocolate or whatever pleases us.

It is not always easy to see things in a new way. Nicodemus did not find it simple, and we are not likely to find it easy either. Still, it is worth the effort. Seeing things from a new angle may make a world of difference in our lives.

Do you need to see something in your life from a different angle?

A SOLITARY CHRISTMAS

Arise, shine; for your light has come,
> and the glory of the LORD has risen upon you.
For darkness shall cover the earth,
> and thick darkness the peoples;
but the LORD will arise upon you,
> and his glory will appear over you.
Nations shall come to your light,
> and kings to the brightness of your dawn.

ISAIAH 60:1-3

I didn't want to hear this passage very much one Christmas season. Due to a variety of circumstances I was going to be spending Christmas by myself that year, something I'd never done before. And I was not happy about it. I complained to my spiritual director about the upcoming lonely holiday and was surprised when she told me of a Christmas she had spent alone, one she'd actually enjoyed. I was expecting sympathy for the darkness of my world, and I was given light instead.

So I began to manufacture a bright side to my Christmas alone. I envisioned it as a day of prayer and attentiveness to the real meaning of the season: the coming of light to our lives. In truth, I worked really hard at convincing myself that it would be a good experience, that I was tired and could use a restful day, though I didn't actually believe myself. I planned to sleep late, spend some time in prayer, and cook myself a good meal. On Christmas Eve I went to church, came home, and prepared to be cheerful the next day, like it or not.

Much to my surprise, it was a wonderful day. I enjoyed the slow and leisurely pace more than the frantic holiday celebrations that sometimes occur. I spent some much needed time in prayer and meditation, had a lovely meal, read, listened to music, called family members long-distance, and generally enjoyed myself. I have spent other holidays alone since then, by choice and not by circumstance.

We can reinvent our holidays in many ways. I have friends who like to invite a group of their single friends over for a holiday, and friends who like to spend a holiday helping others less fortunate than they are. The holidays, with their Norman Rockwell–family images, are sometimes hard for singles who are not close to family. But they can be reshaped, and in the process of refashioning them, perhaps we will find ourselves a little closer to God.

What holiday would you like to refashion for yourself?

EAT DESSERT FIRST

While he was at Bethany in the house of Simon the leper, as he sat at the table, a woman came with an alabaster jar of very costly ointment of nard, and she broke open the jar and poured the ointment on his head. But some were there who said to one another in anger, "Why was the ointment wasted in this way? For this ointment could have been sold for more than three hundred denarii, and the money given to the poor." And they scolded her. But Jesus said, "Let her alone; why do you trouble her? She has performed a good service for me. For you always have the poor with you, and you can show kindness to them whenever you wish; but you will not always have me."

MARK 14:3–7

You've probably heard the proverb "Life is short—eat dessert first." Now, I don't think Jesus says this to those who criticize the woman who anoints him, but perhaps there is an element of it in there somewhere. Jesus tells the angry people that he will not always be with them, that this woman has done him a great kindness that will not be possible later. "Don't wait," he tells them. "You will not always have this opportunity."

That applies to each of us as well. Sometimes we spend years unconsciously waiting for someone or something that signals us to start living our lives, and for many of us that signal will never come from external sources. I remember waking up one day in my mid-thirties and wondering why I was waiting to buy nice furniture, dishes I liked, and other household items. Unconsciously I had been waiting until I married to receive those items. I had put my life on hold without even thinking about it. The house was not magically furnished that day, but over the next few years I began to buy the kinds of dishes I wanted and other household items that grown-ups buy. I had finally realized that life is short and that opportunities slip by when we do not avail ourselves of them.

Jesus' praise of the woman who anoints his head with oil is not an invitation to rampant materialism, but Jesus does not suggest that we never indulge in the good things God has created. The world is full of wonderful things, many of them given to us by God, and sometimes we are the only ones preventing ourselves from enjoying them.

Have you put something in your life on hold?

GOD HEARS

[Jesus] said, "In a certain city there was a judge who neither feared God nor had respect for people. In that city there was a widow who kept coming to him and saying, 'Grant me justice against my opponent.' For a while he refused; but later he said to himself, 'Though I have no fear of God and no respect for anyone, yet because this widow keeps bothering me, I will grant her justice, so that she may not wear me out by continually coming.'" And the Lord said, "Listen to what the unjust judge says. And will not God grant justice to his chosen ones who cry to him day and night?"

LUKE 18:2–7

You've got to love this widow for her gumption. She knows what she wants and needs, and she relentlessly pursues it. The judge tells her no over and over again, but she finally wears him down and is given justice. God will all the more quickly give us what we need, we are told. We need only ask for help.

But as much as I admire the widow, it has been my own experience that God does not immediately grant me whatever I want. I remember asking God for many things that were never given. I asked for the "Right One" to come along or for a bad relationship to continue just so I could stay involved. Though there have been many wonderful relationships in my life, I have never found any that made sense for the long haul. God did not give me what I thought I needed. Then again, perhaps it is like the child who wants a cookie. "I NEED a cookie," he says, rather than "I want a cookie." And when I look back on my life, I see that God has given me all that I need. I have a life I truly enjoy, friends I treasure, the occasional romance, and a career that I love. Maybe God saw the need underneath my want and gave me what I needed—a rich and full life for which I am most grateful. Maybe God heard my demands, as the judge heard the widow's demands, and gave me what was right and just after all.

How has God responded to the needs in your life?

WORKING

> Moses' father-in-law said to him, "What you are
> doing is not good. You will surely wear yourself out,
> both you and these people with you. For the task is
> too heavy for you; you cannot do it alone."
>
> EXODUS 18:17–18

In this scene from Exodus, Moses' father-in-law, Jethro, has found Moses in the desert trying to be everything to everybody. His advice is sound: You cannot do it all alone. Delegate some of the work and let others help you. I wish I had someone like Jethro around me when I act like Moses.

Sometimes we try to be superhuman. We work hard at our jobs. We come home, clean the house, and take care of chores and, for some of us, children. We try to get in a few projects in the evenings, balancing that with our social life and other obligations. If we had the option, we would choose a thirty-six-hour day just so we could get more done. Those are the times when we most need Jethro's advice.

I often feel that I need to be completely self-sufficient, that I shouldn't ask for help. *I can do it all. There is absolutely nothing wrong with me, and I'll prove it to you.* For my trouble, I get overly tired, stressed, irritable, and frustrated. I'm no good for myself or for others. Perhaps I should tape Jethro's words someplace prominent in my office or home and try to remember that I cannot, and need not, do it all alone.

How do you balance work and the rest of your life?

VICTIMHOOD VS. TAKING CONTROL

My child, if you accept my words
    and treasure up my commandments within you,
making your ear attentive to wisdom
    and inclining your heart to understanding;
if you indeed cry out for insight,
    and raise your voice for understanding;
if you seek it like silver,
    and search for it as for hidden treasures—
then you will understand the fear of the LORD
    and find the knowledge of God.

                              PROVERBS 2:1-5

Like most people, I get caught up in feeling like a victim some days. We all carry around bits of painful baggage, and sometimes it gets the better of us. For me it appears when I am sick or particularly tired. I have a bad habit of deciding that if no one is going to take care of me, then I won't take care of myself. I end up like a martyr, wearing my illness, struggle, or exhaustion openly and being a nuisance to myself and those around me. It took me years to learn to stop this behavior when it begins and either ask for help or take the rest, nourishment, or recreation that I need.

Victimhood is a choice. We either choose to remain miserable and live with the depletion of energy and loneliness this induces, or we choose to take control and live otherwise. Cry out for insight and understanding, Proverbs tells us. Seek it—actively—as you would search for buried treasure. There will always be difficulties to be faced in being single, just as there are hard parts of being married. But great treasures exist within the single life, and all it takes is a willingness to locate them.

Are you willing to search for the treasures in the single life? If not, why not?

THROW A PARTY

On the third day there was a wedding in Cana of
Galilee, and the mother of Jesus was there. Jesus and
his disciples had also been invited to the wedding.

JOHN 2:1-2

Sometimes I find it hard to read about weddings,
in the Bible or elsewhere. It isn't that I wish to be married,
but when I read of weddings I am reminded how few celebrations there are in the life of single people. We have no
wedding showers, no baby showers, no weddings, no an-
niversaries that fill our houses with towels, dishes, and all the
things grown-ups are supposed to have. But far more than
the loss of the things people accumulate during these events,
we have few built-in community celebrations of milestones
in our lives. If we have them, often we must orchestrate the
events ourselves.

I remember the freedom I felt when I finally decided that
I was going to throw a birthday party for myself. It was my
thirty-ninth birthday, and I invited a whole house full of
friends over for dinner. It was a wonderful night, full of
laughter and merriment. It was the night I realized it was a
grand thing to throw a party for myself, to invite my friends

to celebrate my existence with me. There may never be any religious ceremonies—weddings and such—that celebrate my existence. But just living on this earth is reason enough to celebrate, and I do not need to wait for anyone to give me permission to do so.

How can you celebrate your life?

BURNOUT

As they came from their mother's womb, so they
shall go again, naked as they came; they shall take
nothing for their toil, which they may carry away
with their hands.

ECCLESIASTES 5:15

I love my work, but I easily forget that it is not the
sum total of who I am. At times I work far too many hours,
too many days in a row, and let the other parts of my life go.
It can be extraordinarily satisfying to get so much done. It
can also lead to complete burnout.

When we work ourselves this hard, life becomes unbalanced. Our body and soul grow unhealthy as we focus all of
our attention on achievement, on proving our worth by how
hard we work and how much we accomplish. In the long run,
working that hard and playing so little leaves me empty and
exhausted, and none the richer in any way. As Ecclesiastes
says, we gain nothing through our toil that we can take with
us. Life is more than the sum of what we complete at work.

Years ago I experienced complete burnout at work, and
even then I couldn't let go of work-as-identity. In my exhaustion, I wanted to cling to the work I understood, which seemed
to give me the sole source of my value. Slowly, however, I

learned to let go and find other things I enjoyed. Not all at once, but a little bit at a time, I trimmed the number of hours I worked a week. One activity at a time, I added other things besides work to my schedule. Finally, I learned to add quiet, rest, time alone, and space for refreshment. It took awhile, and it was not an easy process, but I am a better—and happier—person for the struggle. As the old saying goes, you can't take it with you. You might as well go out and have some fun while you can. No one ever died wishing they had worked harder.

How hard are you working?

DATING

> Raphael said to the young man, "Brother Tobias."
> "Here I am," he answered. Then Raphael said to
> him, "We must stay this night in the home of Raguel.
> He is your relative, and he has a daughter named
> Sarah. He has no male heir and no daughter except
> Sarah only, and you, as next of kin to her, have before
> all other men a hereditary claim on her.... Moreover,
> the girl is sensible, brave, and very beautiful, and
> her father is a good man." . . . Then Tobias said in
> answer to Raphael, "Brother Azariah, I have heard
> that she already has been married to seven husbands
> and that they died in the bridal chamber."
>
> TOBIT 6:11–12, 14

Don't you just love it when friends match you up with a blind date? Of course the date is sensible, brave, and beautiful, or some other list of wonderful qualities. Then you meet the person and discover that he or she isn't the love of your life that your friends promised. Sometimes things do work out, as they did for Tobit. Seven husbands had been killed on their wedding nights by demons, but Raphael gives Tobit objects that protect him. Finally the demons leave him and Sarah. It is an original happy ending in the Bible.

Usually we go on the date with amazing expectations and hopes but find ourselves disappointed when, once again, the perfect person is not seated opposite us over dinner. Dating is so much work! Some dates who have not been the "Right One" for me, however, have become good friends. One of my closest friends came to me this way. Once I got over my initial disappointment that this person wasn't going to make a wonderful romantic partner, I spent time getting to know him, and we have been fast friends for many years. And a dear friend is far more valuable to me than a failed romance.

Have you ever resented a date for not being who you hoped he or she would be?

SEX

Come, my beloved,
　　let us go forth into the fields,
　　and lodge in the villages;
let us go out early to the vineyards,
　　and see whether the vines have budded,
whether the grape blossoms have opened
　　and the pomegranates are in bloom.
There I will give you my love.

SONG OF SOLOMON 7:11–12

We are all sexual beings. Just because we are single does not mean that we have no interest in sex. Even if we could magically turn off our own desires, our culture continually presents us with new images. In ads, movies, books, and other media, sexuality surrounds us, telling us forcefully that sex should be uppermost in our mind.

Though the media often paints a distorted picture of sex, there is nothing wrong with the healthy expression of our sexuality. Being single does not mean that we wear blinders, that we don't notice an attractive man or woman, that this doesn't elicit a response from us. To turn off our responses, to fail to admit that we have them, or to repress them fiercely denies the wholeness of the person created by God. Each of us needs to make decisions about what forms of expression keep us whole, what types of activity are helpful, not harmful, to ourselves and perhaps a partner. We needn't end up in bed with anyone or everyone who attracts us, but to fail to at least delight in the attraction is to give back one of God's great gifts.

How can you more fully recognize your sexuality as a blessing from God?

VACATIONS

The LORD is my shepherd, I shall not want.
    He makes me lie down in green pastures;
he leads me beside still waters;
    he restores my soul.
He leads me in right paths
    for his name's sake.

PSALM 23:1–3

We all need a vacation once in a while, a time to restore body and soul and walk beside still waters and relax. Some people, however, put off taking a vacation. I've been guilty of that myself. Maybe we don't have anyone to go with. Maybe our best times for vacation fall in an odd part of the year, or perhaps our friends aren't interested in the same type of vacation that interests us. For whatever reason, it is easy to fall prey to simply working, avoiding the time away that we need if we are to keep body and soul together.

When I get in this bind, sometimes the solution is taking a retreat or a pilgrimage with others. Going away to a beautiful location or a foreign country with a group of people who begin as strangers and end up as friends enriches my social and spiritual life. Away from ringing phones, E-mail, and other distractions of daily life, we explore aspects of God's creation and pray and play together. I can do this without the dangers of traveling alone. Since meals and accommodations are usually handled by the group's leader, I am free to really enjoy myself. These experiences also meet my need for some social time, and often as not, God's hopes and plans for me come out of the mouth of my companions.

When was your last vacation?

GOOD SOIL

"Listen! A sower went out to sow. And as he sowed,
some seed fell on the path, and the birds came and
ate it up. Other seed fell on rocky ground, where
it did not have much soil, and it sprang up quickly,
since it had no depth of soil. And when the sun
rose, it was scorched; and since it had no root, it
withered away. Other seed fell among thorns, and
the thorns grew up and choked it, and it yielded no
grain. Other seed fell into good soil and brought
forth grain, growing up and increasing and yielding
thirty and sixty and a hundredfold."

MARK 4:3–8

There are many ways to respond to being single;
most of them are contained in this parable about the seed. We
can respond to being single by becoming un-single as rapidly
as possible. We fall on the path only briefly and are quickly
eaten up by something else if we have any choice about it. Or,
rather than actually enjoying our life, we pretend that we are
happy being alone. When we do that, the soil is too thin, and
we wither rapidly. Others of us fall among the thorns, the culture around us that chokes us and tells us being single is a poor
option. Strangled by the thorns, life is often sad and difficult.

Unlike the seed, which must live where it is tossed, we have a choice about where to land. We can choose to be the seed that falls onto good soil and thrives. We can explore our life as single people, mine the riches of it, and learn whatever lessons it has to teach us. By giving of ourselves we can contribute our time, attention, and talents to a needy world and yield thirty and sixty and a hundredfold. By choosing good soil and bringing forth good grain out of our lives, we add so much not only to our own existence but also to the world at large.

Where do you want to grow?

CHAPTER SEVEN
THE NEW JERUSALEM

ENJOYMENT

> Then I saw a new heaven and a new earth; for the
> first heaven and the first earth had passed away, and
> the sea was no more. And I saw the holy city, the new
> Jerusalem, coming down out of heaven from God.
>
> REVELATION 21:1–2

The new Jerusalem, we are told in Revelation, will come down from heaven someday, and things will be different. The streets will be paved with gold. We will enter the city through pearly gates, reminiscent of Matthew's pearl of great worth. Night and darkness will be no more. For some of us, learning to enjoy the life we have is a little like finally entering the new Jerusalem.

There is, after all, so much in which to rejoice. We enjoy tremendous freedoms not available to everyone. Many of us orchestrate a life of our own choosing, one that has fewer compromises than others might make. We don't have to worry about anyone else's career or about growing in ways someone else will find difficult. No one minds if we leave the cap off the toothpaste, and no one notices if we have a conversation with the dog. There is a little bit of the new Jerusalem in our celebration of the single life. The real new Jerusalem may be in the future, but we can enjoy this little piece of it for now.

What in life brings you joy?

LIVING ALONE

Make me to know your ways, O Lord;
  teach me your paths.
Lead me in your truth, and teach me,
  for you are the God of my salvation;
  for you I wait all day long.

PSALM 25:4-5

One of the things I like about living alone is that I have more control over my schedule than those who live in families. If I want to spend an entire day in meditation and prayer—if I want to wait for God all day long—I can do that. I don't have to arrange it with a spouse or children. Friends of mine who are married, particularly those with children, find it much harder to carve out the physical space and quiet they desire for their prayer life. Their quiet moments are relegated to the early hours of the morning or late at night, when there are fewer demands on them.

I can't orchestrate all my time. After all, I have to work for a living and I have commitments, too, but in general I have more control over my time than most couples. I can go home to a quiet house at the end of the day or reserve a weekend for myself, and no one minds—not even the cat. I can spend the best part of my day with God in prayer, rather than give God the moments on which no one else has dibs.

Where does prayer fit into your schedule?

HOUSEKEEPING, OR NOT

Now as they went on their way, he entered a certain village, where a woman named Martha welcomed him into her home. She had a sister named Mary, who sat at the Lord's feet and listened to what he was saying. But Martha was distracted by her many tasks; so she came to him and asked, "Lord, do you not care that my sister has left me to do all the work by myself? Tell her then to help me."

LUKE 10:38–40

With all due apologies to Martha, this passage reminds me of a great joy of living alone: keeping my house as I wish.

A friend's husband died recently, and she is rediscovering this as well. Though she grieves deeply, she also recognizes the need to move on with her life. So she has been rearranging the house, buying new bedroom linens, and making the home into her own again. She has even had some structural work done, removing things that her husband wanted and that she had never liked.

This is one of the great joys of living by ourselves. We can clean as and how we wish, have furniture and things that we like around us. The house can be loud or quiet, whatever suits us. No one checks up on us, and no one makes us clean our room before going to bed. There is no one to care if the dinner dishes don't go in the dishwasher right this minute. Mary and Martha didn't have that choice, and to be truthful, I'm not sure which one I would have been in the story. I am just as likely to want to sit and hear what Jesus is saying as I am to be distracted by a mess that needs cleaning. But I enjoy living in my own home where I am the one to decide whether I will be Mary or Martha today.

Are you more like Mary or Martha?

CHILDREN

Sing, O barren one who did not bear;
    burst into song and shout,
    you who have not been in labor!
For the children of the desolate woman will be more
    than the children of her that is married, says the LORD.

ISAIAH 54:1

Asingle friend of mine loves children but has never found a man she wishes to marry. She has more children in her life, however, than any married person I know. She is a youth leader in her church and is loved by the children and teens. She is active in community service, and the circle of those she loves and cares for is wider than it would ever be if she needed to focus on her own family.

My friend is far from being the desolate barren woman described above. In biblical times a woman without children, particularly male children, had no place in society and no future. Today, though there are still pressures upon women to have children, more options exist, and people without children live full lives. Moreover, many people—children and adults—need the love of those who are childless or whose children are grown. Those of us without spouses and children at home may have time, energy, and love that we are willing to spend on those who need our attention: the hungry or homeless, the dying, the abused. Because our time and energy are not automatically allocated to a family, we might have more love to share with a wider variety of God's children. We may, in fact, have many more "children" than the married person will ever have.

Are you drawn to certain types of God's children? How are you finding ways to include them in your life?

MALE AND FEMALE

So God created humankind in his image,
in the image of God he created them;
male and female he created them.

GENESIS 1:27

God created us in God's own image. Apparently both male and female are in the image of God. One benefit of being single is the opportunity to explore both our male and our female sides—all the aspects of God within us.

When I was a schoolchild, one of my great frustrations was that girls took home economics and boys took shop. Period. So when I became an adult living on my own, I was helpless with household projects. And I've known many a man who couldn't sew a button back on his shirt. Being single, and particularly living alone, provides us with an opportunity to explore those tasks and personality characteristics we normally associate with someone of the opposite sex. For instance, I've learned a great deal about managing my own money, and a male friend of mine is a wonderful cook. Professionally and personally I've had to learn to be strong and stand up for myself. Men, on the other hand, have an opportunity to explore their softer side, to learn to cry when they need to. Without a partner to assume some of these tasks and roles, we have an opportunity to explore more aspects of ourselves and our abilities.

Is there a side of you that needs exploring?

FREEDOM

I want you to be free from anxieties. The unmarried
man is anxious about the affairs of the Lord, how
to please the Lord; but the married man is anxious
about the affairs of the world, how to please his wife,
and his interests are divided. And the unmarried
woman and the virgin are anxious about the affairs
of the Lord, so that they may be holy in body and
spirit; but the married woman is anxious about the
affairs of the world, how to please her husband.

1 CORINTHIANS 7:32-34

Paul, the author of 1 Corinthians, wrote a lot about
marriage, divorce, and singleness. Scholars have spent cen-
turies arguing about his views, trying to interpret them, and
applying them to life today. Those debates aside, Paul holds
up an important truth about the single life in this passage.
There is a great freedom for single people in that we don't
have to worry about obligations to spouse and family. We
have the freedom to live differently from those who must take
family into account when making decisions.

One of the things I enjoy most about living singly is that I
can be more spontaneous in my plans than my married
friends. I can say yes or no to an invitation based on my own

preferences, without consulting anyone. I can travel on my own schedule. My leisure time is my own, and I spend it as I wish or need because that time does not belong to a spouse or family. I can also spend time in prayer without having to carve out space and time in the midst of a busy household.

Sometimes I worry that this seems selfish, but a good friend reminded me that people enter into lifetime relationships for selfish reasons too. They must get as much as they give to a relationship, or it will fail. For them, that is just good self-care, just as my enjoyment of my own freedom and the ability to use it wisely helps me take care of me.

Do you give yourself permission to enjoy the freedoms of the single life?

TRAVEL

> So, being sent out by the Holy Spirit, they [Paul and
> Barnabas] went down to Seleucia; and from there
> they sailed to Cyprus. When they arrived at Salamis,
> they proclaimed the word of God in the synagogues
> of the Jews.
>
> ACTS 13:4-5

Paul traveled constantly, preaching the Word around
the ancient world, something that would have been much
harder had he been married with a family. The same was true
for the Old Testament prophets Jeremiah and Elijah.

Not everyone enjoys traveling alone, but for some it can
be wonderfully liberating. For many years I worked in a job
where I was too busy to take a vacation in the summer. The
best time for me to go was always in March—not the most
popular vacation time for most people. Sometimes I found a
friend who wanted to travel somewhere with me at that time
of year, but often I ventured forth on my own, visiting friends
around the country or just going someplace I wanted to go.

Traveling alone entails a magnificent freedom. You can go
where you want, on your own timetable. No one minds if you
sleep late or get going at the crack of dawn. If you see a side
trip that looks interesting, you can take it. You can stop when

you want, go when you are ready, and follow where the Spirit leads. Traveling alone does not mean that you are without companionship either, since there are always interesting people to meet on the road. And just like Paul, you can visit places where old friends wait to greet you.

Does anything prevent you from
traveling alone?

SATURDAY MORNING

This is the day that the LORD has made;
   let us rejoice and be glad in it.

PSALM 118:24

One of the best times of the week, for me, is Saturday morning. It is the one day when I can sleep late and have a leisurely morning, uninterrupted by computers, phones, people, or noise. Whenever I can, I sleep until I am ready to get up. Then I make myself a cup of my favorite coffee, climb back into bed, coffee in hand, and read a good book for a couple of hours. Sometimes the cat comes and curls up next to me, but aside from that I am alone and the house is quiet. This is the time I value the most.

Many writers have pointed out in recent years that solitude is not the same thing as loneliness. Saturday mornings are about that pregnant solitude for me. My week is full of people, phone calls, E-mail, chores, and activities of all sorts. On Saturday morning, all is banished, and I spend a few hours with myself and do as I please. It is, for me, one of the great extravagances of the single life. Saturday morning is the time when I am most aware of the wonderful day that God has made, the day when I am most ready to rejoice.

What activity helps you rejoice in one of God's days?

FLIRTATION

I compare you, my love,
    to a mare among Pharaoh's chariots.
Your cheeks are comely with ornaments,
    your neck with strings of jewels.
We will make you ornaments of gold,
    studded with silver.

SONG OF SOLOMON 1:9–11

Flirtations are fun. Some people in Christian history have tried to sanitize Song of Solomon by saying the writing reflects God's love for Israel. But the language is too vivid, too concrete for it to be a metaphor. God created us to be attracted to one another, and saying so in ways that are funny or flattering or clever is simply a reflection of the joy God implanted in us.

Flirtations can be used in ways that are harmful, certainly. People are hurt when the receiving party understands the flattery in a different way than it was meant. A good line or "feminine wiles" can be used to gain power, rather than truly express affection. But real, genuine flattery—that which expresses appreciation and admiration—is a great joy to give and receive. That kind of flattery is modeled wonderfully for us in Song of Solomon. Let us not be afraid to brighten someone's day, to express our affection for others, or to receive compliments from others. It is part of the joy that God intends for each of us.

Who in your life could use a little affection?

BE HERE NOW

For everything there is a season, and a time for every
  matter under heaven:
a time to be born, and a time to die;
a time to plant, and a time to pluck up what is planted.

ECCLESIASTES 3:1-2

A friend of mine in her early thirties really wanted to be married someday, but she knew marriage was not on the immediate horizon. She wasn't in a serious relationship of any sort, and she didn't see one coming around the next corner. She had a couple of choices: She could mourn what wasn't, or she could enjoy the life she had. She chose to enjoy her life as it existed at that moment and to worry about what wasn't another day. Her life was rich and full, with many friends and lots of wonderful opportunities, and that was enough for the time being. She got married a few years later, but she had truly enjoyed her single time.

Enjoying life as it is today does not mean that we would not welcome a change in the future. There is, as Ecclesiastes tells us, a time for everything. Our lives can be full of friends and travel and careers today, and full of family and children and other opportunities tomorrow. We do not need to feel that because today is good, we have no dreams for a different life next month or next year. But we do a great disservice to ourselves when we fail to enjoy what we have at the moment because only our dreams of tomorrow will make us happy. "Be here now," many of the great Eastern philosophies tell us, and Ecclesiastes says the same thing. Dream all you want—your life will be filled with many different opportunities, and what you have right now is one of them.

What is it time to do today?

CHAPTER EIGHT
GOD'S UNCONDITIONAL LOVE

GOD'S LOVE

Now when all the people were baptized, and when
Jesus also had been baptized and was praying, the
heaven was opened, and the Holy Spirit descended
upon him in bodily form like a dove. And a voice
came from heaven, "You are my Son, the Beloved;
with you I am well pleased."

LUKE 3:21–22

As Jesus is baptized, we hear God saying to Jesus,
"You are my Son, the Beloved; with you I am well pleased"
(Lk 3:22). God does not say, "You are my Son, the Beloved—
now when are you going to settle down, get married, and give
me some grandchildren?" God's declaration of love for Jesus
comes before Jesus begins his public ministry. It does not de-
pend on Jesus' being successful or doing a good job. It does
not come with strings attached or with a caveat that says,
"But I'll love you better when . . ." God loves us that way too.
Each and every one of us, individually. Not for what we've
done or who we will marry. God loves us "as is."

Do you believe that God loves you "as is"?

GOD CALLS US BY NAME

But now thus says the LORD,
 he who created you, O Jacob,
 he who formed you, O Israel:
Do not fear, for I have redeemed you;
 I have called you by name, you are mine.
When you pass through the waters, I will be with you;
 and through the rivers, they shall not overwhelm
 you;
when you walk through fire you shall not be burned,
 and the flame shall not consume you.

          ISAIAH 43:1–2

I first heard this passage in the midst of a difficult time in my life. In the middle of my darkness, a friend read it to me as a reminder of God's presence and promise. God, who formed us, calls us by name and promises to be with us no matter what. We will walk through trouble, flame, and water and not be overwhelmed by any of it. I found great comfort in these words.

Recently I talked with a friend who is newly divorced after a long marriage. In his late fifties, he is amazed to be single again; this was never a part of his life's plan. After being married all of his adult life, he faces a whole new world and is finding it difficult to be single within the church, which, at best, has mixed feelings about his divorce. He will go through some darkness, I suspect, before he finds the light again. When I hold him in my prayers I remember this passage from Isaiah for him. As God did for me in my distress, God will guide my friend through the deep waters and the fire, and he will not be overwhelmed. God calls him, as God calls all of us, by name, and we are redeemed.

How has God guided you through the water and the fire?

A STRONGHOLD IN TIMES OF TROUBLE

The LORD is a stronghold for the oppressed,
   a stronghold in times of trouble.
And those who know your name put their trust
      in you,
   for you, O LORD, have not forsaken those who
      seek you.

PSALM 9:9–10

A friend of mine and his wife lived in an apartment complex, and a newly divorced friend of theirs needed to find a new home. When my friend went to the landlord and asked for an application for his friend, the landlord told him that he didn't accept single tenants. To this landlord, single tenants were young and loud, threw parties every night, lived the wild life, and disturbed everyone else.

Aside from the discrimination, which is troubling, I am even more disturbed that someone believes that there is a "typical" single. We are many different people, each of us unique. Some of us are eighteen and free of many responsibilities, while others are single parents. There are divorced singles, and those who have lost their spouses to death. There are forty-year-old, never-married, single professionals, and many others. To lump us all together in a stereotype is not only unfair, it flies in the face of what the Bible says about God's love for each of us as unique people. But that God loves me unconditionally for just who I am is a great source of strength for me, especially when others fail to recognize my uniqueness. God is my stronghold in times of trouble.

How is God a stronghold for you in times of trouble?

THE BODY HOLY

Do you not know that you are God's temple and that
God's Spirit dwells in you?

1 CORINTHIANS 3:16

I am God's temple. This body that I walk around in,
with all its splendor and flaws, is God's temple. God dwells
within me, not just in an abstract way, but in my actual flesh
and bones. Because God dwells within me, I—body and soul
—am holy.

Yeah, right. Our culture does not teach us to understand
our bodies as enfleshed holiness. We are taught to use our
bodies for flirting, for attracting potential lovers. If we are unhappy with our bodies, we learn to hide them in nondescript
clothing designed to deflect attention. No matter what kind
of body we live in, we wish it were bigger here or smaller
there, or just different somehow. We do not see our bodies,
or our beings in total, as God's temple. We are perpetually
dissatisfied with what God has made in us.

When I first read this passage many years ago, I found it
such a powerful thought that I copied it and taped it up on
my mirror. Every day as I brushed my teeth or combed my
hair, I read that I was God's temple and that God's Spirit
dwelt in me. Over time, I came to trust that promise. Imagine

what it would be like for you to believe for a day, or even an hour, that you are God's temple, that God's Spirit dwells within you, and that this makes you holy.

Do you believe you are God's temple?

WORM THEOLOGY

But I am a worm, and not human;
    scorned by others, and despised by the people.

PSALM 22:6

A friend of mine grew up with a theology that is simply stated: We are all worms. We are all unworthy. It is, therefore, improper to accept compliments, to speak of anything of which we are proud, or to think anything much of ourselves.

When I combine that bit of theology with the negative feelings many people have about singles, I wonder how singles survive. Advertisers and marketing folks make their living by trying to convince us that we might be worms now but that they can provide something that will make us princes and princesses. Buy the right stuff, they say to us, and you will not be worms any longer. For singles, that message sometimes gets turned into: Buy the right stuff, and you will find the person who wants to marry you. Marry the right person, and you will become fully human. Life's problems are solved.

But God's truth is that we are not worms, that there is no one right way to live, no goal toward which we strive where the prize is becoming human rather than worm. We have a natural tendency to look at others and think that they have discovered the secret of happiness. The truth is that they have good days and bad days, just like we do. They have some of life figured out, and so do we. The journey is the key issue here, and the fact that we are always on the journey, always searching and exploring, does not make us worms wiggling in the dirt. God loves us as we are and rejoices with us when we actually enjoy the ride.

Is it easier for you to believe that you are a worm or that you are God's beloved?

LIGHT OF THE WORLD

"You are the light of the world. A city built on a hill cannot be hid. No one after lighting a lamp puts it under the bushel basket, but on the lampstand, and it gives light to all in the house. In the same way, let your light shine before others, so that they may see your good works and give glory to your Father in heaven."

MATTHEW 5:14–16

We singles can far too easily hide our light. Being solo in a couples' world, we often feel conspicuous when we do things alone. We slink into movie theaters and hope we don't see anyone we know. We go out to dinner in a restaurant alone and bring a newspaper or book to hide behind. Worse yet, sometimes we don't even bother going out, since by going out alone we only call attention to the fact that we are by ourselves.

We do a great disservice to ourselves and God, however, when we hide. By putting our lamps—ourselves—under a bushel basket we say that what God created is not good after all. But there is no question that each of us is a shining lamp. Matthew does not say, "If you have a light, let it shine." He says, "Let your light shine." When we hide, we deny the gospel and say that our lamp is defective, that we have nothing to offer. By hiding our light we fail to give God glory. It is tempting to believe that we are not valuable because there is only one of us. Then again, who are we to argue with God when we are told that we are—each one of us—the light of the world?

What prevents you from letting your light shine?

GOD'S LOVE EMPOWERS

"Abide in me as I abide in you. Just as the branch
cannot bear fruit by itself unless it abides in the
vine, neither can you unless you abide in me."

JOHN 15:4

Years ago I had a married friend whom I admired
greatly. She and her husband were extraordinarily loving
people, always giving of themselves to everyone around them.
By comparison, I saw myself as much less giving, much less loving, and I consoled myself by reasoning that her ability to love
others came from the deep love she and her husband shared.

A few years later, her husband died, and she has remained
single since that time. She is still generous and gracious. The
loss of her husband did not change who she is. I realized that it
is God's love, not her husband's, that my friend reflects for the
rest of the world to see. Realizing that helped me to stop waiting for some person to love me as much as God does. It freed
me to begin to live out God's love for me in my own world.

"Abide in me as I abide in you," Jesus says in John 15:4. We
cannot bear fruit—cannot love others and bring joy into the
world—unless we abide in the vine. Once we live in God's
love, however, our lives become rich and full, and we need
nothing more to complete us.

Are you waiting to be part of a couple before living out God's love for you?

CLAIMING GOD'S LOVE

The earth is the LORD's and all that is in it,
   the world, and those who live in it.

PSALM 24:1

We are God's, this psalm tells us. Genesis says that God viewed creation and called it good. Which means that, as part of God's creation, we are good and we are loved by God. All of us have been told that, and theoretically we believe it, but how many of us can really claim it out loud and not feel a little squeamish? It took me nearly forty years to do that.

For many of us, perhaps particularly those who have never married or have been divorced, dealing with the feelings of rejection, of being not quite good enough, can get in the way of our relationships with God and the rest of the world. We live, sometimes, with a vague sense that we are failures, that there might be something wrong with us. Reconciling that with the statement that we are God's and that God loves us can seem impossible.

Yet letting God's love in can be one of the most liberating moments of your life. Letting go of the value judgments placed on you and allowing yourself to feel God's love — which has always been with you — is frightening and exhilarating. I remember the first time I admitted out loud that

God loved me. I thought that thunder and lightning were probably going to strike me down. Instead I felt a quiet in my soul that I hadn't known before. The truth is that God loves you, as you are. You are God's. Remember whose you are today, and claim it for yourself. It just might change your life.

What would happen if you admitted, out loud, that God loves you?

GOD, NOT THE KNIGHT ON A WHITE HORSE

Blessed be the LORD,
 for he has heard the sound of my pleadings.
The LORD is my strength and my shield;
 in him my heart trusts;
so I am helped, and my heart exults,
 and with my song I give thanks to him.

PSALM 28:6–7

During my teenage years and many of my adult ones, I spent my days and nights wishing for the "right" person to come along. Someone who would make me whole, who would prevent me from ever being lonely again, someone with whom I would ride off into the sunset and be happy ever after. Nearly everything that was wrong with my world would be solved by finding the "right" person to fill my life.

Over time, I came to understand intellectually that the "right" person wouldn't solve anything in my life, but my heart lagged way behind my head. My heart could not let go of the fairy tale. I felt like a child sitting in a movie theater. While the film played, the world was rosy and wonderful. But if it stopped in the middle, if the spell was broken, I was left sitting in the dark, alone and surrounded by nothingness.

My heart caught up to my head only when I finally realized that God loves me. God not only loves me but does so deeply and unconditionally. God heard the sound of my pleadings all those years and responded over and over with love until I heard. I no longer needed the "right" person to heal my life. God is now and forever my strength and my shield, "so I am helped, and my heart exults, and with my song I give thanks to him" (Ps 28:7).

How does God answer your pleadings?

OPPORTUNITIES

The word that came to Jeremiah from the LORD:
"Come, go down to the potter's house, and there
I will let you hear my words." So I went down to
the potter's house, and there he was working at his
wheel. The vessel he was making of clay was spoiled
in the potter's hand, and he reworked it into another
vessel, as seemed good to him.

JEREMIAH 18:1–4

I know many people who think of themselves as the clay spoiled in the potter's hands. Some of my divorced friends, in particular, think of themselves this way. Others, single all of their lives, suffer the same fear. They know no other reason why they are still single.

We all feel like this at times, particularly when life throws us a curve of some kind. We'd planned one kind of life, and we got another. We had planned to be married to this person for the rest of our life, but one day they asked for a divorce, and we felt rejected, like spoiled clay. But from that piece of clay can come something wonderful, something unexpected and good. I do not believe that God brings difficulty into our life in order to make us pliable enough to mold us into something completely different. I do think that the hardships of life often contain doors and windows to new vistas, new opportunities. If we are willing, God will be with us as we walk through those doors. God, like the potter, will lay hands on us and rework us. It takes courage to trust the process, for we cannot know what we will become. But with God as our partner, we can be assured that it will be something good.

Do you trust the skill of the Potter's hands?

SINGLENESS IN SCRIPTURE

The same day some Sadducees came to him, saying there is no resurrection; and they asked him a question, saying, "Teacher, Moses said, 'If a man dies childless, his brother shall marry the widow, and raise up children for his brother.' Now there were seven brothers among us; the first married, and died childless, leaving the widow to his brother. The second did the same, so also the third, down to the seventh. Last of all, the woman herself died. In the resurrection, then, whose wife of the seven will she be? For all of them had married her."

Jesus answered them, "You are wrong, because you know neither the scriptures nor the power of God. For in the resurrection they neither marry nor are given in marriage, but are like angels in heaven."

MATTHEW 22:23–30

Some would have us believe that there is a biblical mandate to marry. "Be fruitful and multiply," God tells Adam and Eve. To be sure, there are many passages of this sort in the Bible. The culture around us reinforces this message. Some of the biggest movies play on our desire to finally find the right person. Romance means big bucks for movie-makers, publishers, and ad makers. Even psychologists have contributed to this illusion, using models of adult development that assume all or most adults are married.

But the Bible contains other images as well. Paul, one of the most stridently single people in the Bible, prescribes marriage only for those who feel they cannot live a moral life as single people. Then there is this wonderful passage from Matthew, which tells us that in life eternal there is no marriage at all. The angels are all single, as we will be someday.

The truth is that there is no biblical mandate for or against marriage or the single life. It is the quality of our relationships with God and with one another that matters, not our living arrangements. Married and single both, we can be faithful or unfaithful servants of God.

How are you God's faithful servant?

KNOWING FULLY

When I was a child, I spoke like a child, I thought like a child, I reasoned like a child; when I became an adult, I put an end to childish ways. For now we see in a mirror, dimly, but then we will see face to face. Now I know only in part; then I will know fully, even as I have been fully known.

1 CORINTHIANS 13:11–12

I'm glad Paul was confident that he'd reached adulthood and put away his childish ways. At forty-two, I'm not yet clear that I've reached that stage, and I'm pretty sure I haven't put away my childish ways. Still, I understand much more about God and about myself than I did twenty years ago. And I hope to know more about God twenty years from now.

At the age of twenty-two I still assumed that I would be married someday, even though I wasn't sure that was what I wanted. Living a married life, however, was all I could imagine, and I assumed I would do as everyone else did. As time went on and I failed to find a relationship that I thought would stand the test of time, I began to sense that something was wrong with me. I feared I was a failure, and there were days when I felt desperate about my single state. As a few more years passed, I realized that I really enjoyed living alone, and I began to tell my friends that if I ever married, my spouse would have to live in a house next door to me. My sense of myself as a single person has evolved and changed over the years, and my comfort with being single has grown as my knowledge of God's love for me has matured. I saw my life only dimly in my twenties, only I didn't know it. I suspect the same is true even now, in my forties.

> *How has your view of life and God changed over the years?*

GOD LOVES YOU

For you love all things that exist,
and detest none of the things that you have made,
for you would not have made anything if you had
hated it.

WISDOM OF SOLOMON 11:24

Y ou love all things that exist," says Solomon to God.
That includes you and me. Addressing God, Solomon continues: "For you would not have made anything if you had hated it." That last line really grabbed my attention when I read it. "You would not have made anything if you had hated it." That statement is even stronger than the first line. God not only loves all that is created, but we wouldn't have been created in the first place if we weren't worth the trouble.

I remember how shocked I was when I first began to really believe that God loves me. All my life I'd been unable to make that claim. I knew it was true for others, but I couldn't find it within me to say, even silently to myself, that God loves me as I am. And I didn't learn to do that overnight. It took many years, lots of prayer, and the prayers of others for me to finally know —really deep down—that God loves me. When I finally got it, I found a peace in my soul I'd never known. I found the freedom to give up wishing I were someone different. Being able to say to God, and to others, that I know God loves me completely and unconditionally was the single most freeing moment of my life. It was when I understood that wonderful statement that God loves all that exists. "For you would not have made anything if you had hated it."

God loves you, with no ifs, ands, or buts—
do you believe it?